T0090516

"I have known Denise Michel for over 20 years. I didn't know the battles she was dealing with for a long time, but I knew from several mutual friends that she had medical problems.

Through her book "Holographic Tattoo," she leads us on her journey of a series of wins and losses from a physical war in her own body. That is transformational and, on some levels, mystic.

The very word Holographic means to morph from one image to another. A tattoo is a symbol of love, courage, and some instances, defeat. Depending on the person's journey.

In several cultures worldwide, Australian Aborigines, American Indians, and Ninjas have believed in shape-shifting. Denise's journey follows a very symbolic path from a medical journey that takes us on a series of trials to overcome medical conditions that can be extremely overwhelming.

This account beautifully maps out her journey of strength and unending resolve. I am proud of her strength of faith, courage, and perseverance. I am honored to know her as my beautiful friend."

—Pete Spates
Owner, Natural Responses Horsemanship
Cowboy from Jones Creek, TX
International horse trainer

HOLOGRAPHIC
TATTOO
PART ONE

The development of DreamWeaving philosophy
as an integrative health perspective

DENISE M. MICHEL

BALBOA.PRESS
A DIVISION OF HAY HOUSE

Balboa Press books may be ordered through booksellers or by contacting:

Balboa Press
A Division of Hay House
1663 Liberty Drive
Bloomington, IN 47403
www.balboapress.com
844-682-1282

Because of the dynamic nature of the Internet, any web addresses or
links contained in this book may have changed since publication and
may no longer be valid. The views expressed in this work are solely those
of the author and do not necessarily reflect the views of the publisher,
and the publisher hereby disclaims any responsibility for them.

The author of this book does not dispense medical advice or prescribe
the use of any technique as a form of treatment for physical, emotional,
or medical problems without the advice of a physician, either directly
or indirectly. The intent of the author is only to offer information
of a general nature to help you in your quest for emotional and
spiritual well-being. In the event you use any of the information in
this book for yourself, which is your constitutional right, the author
and the publisher assume no responsibility for your actions.

Cover art by Viviana Rivera

Print information available on the last page.

ISBN: 979-8-7652-3991-9 (sc)
ISBN: 979-8-7652-3992-6 (e)

Balboa Press rev. date: 06/06/2023

This book is dedicated to the individuals
who made this book possible

"Amber"   Angela Schmidt
Carrie Calkins   Niki Nicholson
Gloria Ziebell   Jim "Cheekeaux" Michel
Dr. Linda Howe   Dr. Luke Cua
Dr. Mary Smith   Dr. Arti Prasad
Ahma & Bops   Dr. Ben Karas
Jamie Michel   Yolanda Vera
Joel Martinez   Veronica Vigil
Shannon Anthony   Joanna Hurley
Buster Bu Man   Brucie

This book is also dedicated to the loving
memory of the Genuine and Untamable:

Virginia Litza   Kelly Loy
Dr. Sue Brown   Andrea Dewey
Lisa Hannes   Linda Michel
Maha   Ty-chi
Barty Party   Jackie

Contents

Preface

Dear friends and colleagues,

I wrote this book because I developed a way to tap into the body's ability to recover with divine guidance and felt an undeniable desire to share this integrative healing perspective. I learned much during that process as a patient. As a physician, I believe this approach may have the potential to help many people and animals.

Along my journey, there were many instances when I wondered what someone else would have done had they not had the knowledge I'd earned as a physician. I wondered what someone would do if they didn't know they had holistic options. My curiosity about the body/mind/spirit's capacity, my sense of adventure, and a craving for health justice drove me to continue to heal. I decided to share my story.

Since I wanted to teach others what I had learned, I designed this book to align my experiences with the core curriculum for DreamWeaving Holographic Health. DreamWeaving is a holographic perspective of health that aligns with body, mind, emotion, and spirit.

Holographic Health looks at wellness from a diverse, dynamic, and inclusive perspective.

I invite you to experience a holographic wellness perspective and share my journey.

Love and Peace,
Dr. Denise

Acknowledgments

First, I am grateful to the Creator/God for allowing me to experience many nuances of life. I asked for God's grace and guidance to heal. DreamWeaving is the result.

Amber, thank you for courageously giving me aromatherapy treatments and supporting our family physically and financially through challenging times. Thank you for growing, applying your knowledge, and sharing your heart selflessly.

Mom, Gloria Ziebell, thank you for checking in with me regularly and ensuring my family and I always had what we needed. Somehow you intuitively knew when I needed help. Thank you for giving me the gift of travel and for your hospitality. You've been extraordinarily generous without asking anything in return or telling anybody. Thank you, and Ole!

Dad, James Michel, you knew just what to say to keep me on my path. Thank you for encouraging me to believe in myself and live my truth. I appreciate your patience and generosity.

Yolanda Vera, you have been a mentor throughout my life. You are compassionate, creative, innovative, and generous. Thanks to you, Martha Matthews and Annmarette

Vera, for welcoming me into your home. I healed, and my book transformed for many years under your roof.

Niki Nicholson, thank you for bringing the gift of laughter into my life. You are extremely generous, brilliant, and loyal. Carrie Calkins, thank you for your friendship, creativity, generosity, and the remote healing. And Shannon Anthony, I appreciate the DreamWeaving treatments you gave and for continuously encouraging me to finish this book. Each of you consistently showed up for me in ways I will always appreciate and remember. You were relentless with your love, courage, and support and asked nothing in return.

Dr. Luke Cua, your supplement formulas and acupuncture treatments were life-saving. It's an honor to know both you and your wife, Irene. I can't thank you enough for sharing your faith and compassion and applying your centuries-old knowledge so skillfully.

Dr. Arti Prasad, thank you for accepting me as your patient and testing me within my body's parameters. I'm in awe of your palpation skills. You laid the foundation for many tests that were to come. You gave me hope.

Dr. Mary E. Smith, your courage, knowledge, and innovation with integrative healing propelled me forward in health and life. The acupoints you taught me helped me and, consequently, countless people and animals.

To all DreamWeaving Technique & Fitness certified practitioners - *Amber*, Shannon Anthony, Veronica Vigil, Joel Martinez, and HelenLisle. All of you demonstrated grit, determination, and an open mind. Thanks for being such amazing, talented, and beautiful people. To all DreamWeaving students, especially Stephanie Salazar,

Veronica Vigil, Martina, Isabella, and David - thank you for being there so I could do what I love, which is to teach DreamWeaving.

Dr. Linda Howe, you're a beacon of hope for the world. Thank you for guiding me on a path of discovery and development via Akashic Record readings for the logo in the early 2000s, developing a curriculum in 2009, and a life-saving move to Iowa in 2015.

Thank you to the readers of various drafts. *Amber,* Gayla Turner, Dr. Linda Howe, Carrie Calkins, Angela Schmidt, Jamie Michel, and Laura Hurtienne, your comments transformed this book and my perspective on health.

I'm grateful for the many people who took my family and me into their homes and gave us shelter and love. Thank you, Ahma and Bops, I smile thinking of the memories we shared in your home and my nickname. Joanna Hurley, I made pivotal realizations that set the course for my future while staying in your guest house. Thank you all for your hospitality and generosity.

Nathana Bird, thank you for the exciting and enlightening conversations. Brenda G Precious Atencio and Kateri Keevama-Atencio, thank you for checking in on me and offering a sense of belonging. Iona Valdez, thank you for keeping me in your prayers. Your comments had perfect timing, were right on the money, and inspired me to keep on.

Thank you to those who gave their healing talents to me selflessly and generously. Angela Schmidt, you showed up within days of my request for help. You've been a tremendous blessing in my life for decades. Thank you for your encouragement and selfless healing. Lynda and Maria Yraceburu, bringing your class to our home to help me heal was a tremendous honor and blessing. Thank you for the work you do to benefit the entire planet. Kathleen (aka The Sound Lady), thank you for being timely and talented with your gifts. You showed tremendous poise and caring during challenging times. Julie Dewerd, you brought friendship, sustenance, and much-needed nutrition with perfect timing. Thank you.

Virginia Litza profoundly influenced my life, my work, and this book. She introduced me to quality essential oils, shared her holistic healing knowledge, and gifted me with two beautiful dogs, Ty-chi and Buster. Her feedback, enthusiasm, and support of my work influence my life's direction daily.

Kelly Loy's relentless quest to teach and employ holistic healing inspired me. Kelly taught me courage and strength. We often laughed about trials and tribulations and our ability to keep calm and carry on under dire circumstances. True friends like that with shared experiences are few and far between. I feel fortunate to have learned about healing with and beside her.

Dr. Sue Brown introduced me to low and non-force chiropractic. She influenced my understanding of the nervous system, whole health, and teaching style. I learned about tone, rapport, and identifying and releasing patterns within an individual's system. I'm beyond grateful for her work.

Thank you to all my friends, family members, students, and patients for your feedback while I developed my perspective of healing. Your generosity and authenticity continues to inspire me.

Introduction

Everyone has a philosophy they follow. Mine is DreamWeaving Holographic Health. In this book, I share how I developed the philosophy behind DreamWeaving.

Necessity pulsed me toward innovation for survival, health, and wellness. Finding myself in unknown territory with my health, I gathered scientific data and combined it with the ancient wisdom of time-tested traditional healing. When I discovered unity between the complementary concepts, I aligned them and inadvertently embarked on an integrative healing adventure.

Since the body innately restores itself to balance, known as homeostasis, this concept could benefit the overall health of any individual. I do not recommend that you try these techniques for your health unless you consult your physician and are monitored regularly. The main idea I want to share is the process I used to integrate holistic healing with Western Medicine.

I wrote this book while I was still in survival mode. I describe my experiences and share my process. Even though my cognitive function and overall health have improved, I decided not to change how the passages read. It gives the reader an experiential glimpse into my mind and mindset during that time. I aim to promote compassion for individuals who have experienced health challenges and their caregivers.

I hope you find the methods and experiences I share helpful for your health and life. When you have good health, you can live happily, enjoy prosperity, and spend quality time with your family and friends.

SECTION 1

THE SOUL'S WHIP

Recalibrating my compass

Chapter 1

The opportunity to live as a work of
art resides in daily choices.

June 3, 2014
Downtown Albuquerque, NM

The right side of my body is going numb and my face is swelling. I begin to shake.

"Take me to the appointment," I slur to Amber. "They need to see this happen. I'll try to keep myself afloat until we get there. I need help!"

My muscles are weakening and I have difficulty standing. I can't swallow.

I review my actions that morning. *I was typing a list of symptoms for my doctor and moving around fine before I took a shower. I didn't print them out! Think. What do I need to put in this bag? Oils! Clove. We ran out of Helichrysum. Which blends have Helichrysum in them? Trauma Life blend! What else do I need? I feel nauseous now. I might be hungry after this passes. Blueberries, for brain health, and coconut water to take the supplements with. Supplements. I need supplements. Focus!*

Amber helps me into the car.

It feels as if icepicks are jammed into the bridge of my nose and right temple. My vision is blurry. I wince.

I take inventory of my symptoms to share with my doctors. *Ice pick in the chest. Sharp pain clawing in my neck and at the base of my skull. My right ear feels weird. That sharp pain moves to different places throughout my body.*

Where are we going? I remember, my acupuncture appointment at the Integrative Medicine Clinic that I attend. We're running late! I hope this doctor can help me!

I slur my words. "Traffic. Try. Side streets."

We're lost! She's panicking, and my brain, I don't know how long I can teeter on edge like this. I can't swallow. I hope I don't pass out. Focus. Breathe. Remain conscious! Come on. Remain conscious. Breathe.

Chapter 2

Thirty minutes later. At the clinic. In the car.

I feel myself moving in slow motion. My senses feel magnified. The doctor in me tries to remain present and aware of this familiar barrage of symptoms. From that perspective, I feel reverence for this experience of my body's innate wisdom. From my perspective as a patient, I feel terrified and confused.

I notice the tremor in my left hand and cannot move my right arm. Then, I push the passenger door open with my left arm. I whisper to Amber, "Too weak to stand." I slump in the seat. The car door remains ajar.

Panic-stricken, Amber hurries into the clinic. We're twenty-five minutes late. *Here they come with a wheelchair. I don't want to go in a wheelchair. The tone that sets. I'm too young for this to happen.*

I'm wheeled to a treatment room and gently assisted onto a treatment table.

Amber checks me in at the front desk and enters the treatment room. She says to me, "They called 911!" She and I exchange a concerned glance.

There's a slight pause. Amber's eyes are wide. I close mine.

I hold out my right hand, but it doesn't go where I intend it to go. *Come on, hand. Go where I tell you to go. Okay. Focus! This has happened before. I can use my left hand to guide my right hand.*

I say, "My bag. The oils. Clove and Trauma Life."

After a year and a half of trial and error using holistic modalities as palliative care, I'd found a consistent temporary remedy for these events. I'd narrowed my essential oil choices down to two that worked well repeatedly. I chose Clove primarily for its blood thinning and antioxidant properties. I incorporated Helichrysum because it aligns with my cultural background, is traditionally used as an adaptogen for blood and lipids, helps support the nervous system, and has anti-inflammatory properties. This combination of oils temporarily alleviated symptoms for two events earlier this week. And those events had even more intense symptoms. I decided to continue to use what worked in my experience. But, we'd run out of Helichrysum. I worked with the resources we had and used a blend that contained Helichrysum.

Amber asks how many drops of each essential oil I need and expertly allows drops to fall onto the palm of my hand. I slowly rub my hands together, still unable to feel my right hand. Then, my left hand guides the scented palms near my face. I inhale deeply and slowly through my nose and mouth. I stop inhaling as soon as I feel a sharp pain in my abdomen. Instinctively, I sense that I'll be okay. Within a few moments, I'm able to speak in sentences. I am grateful and hope someone will identify these events' root causes.

I'm hyperaware, and sense fear permeating the room. I feel trapped and want to get up. The familiar scent of pain wafts up from my body, coordinating with the increasing intensity of awareness within my body. There's a sharp pain in my neck, back, and chest. It's moving up the left side of my right leg. My head pain is dizzying, and the ever-present burning sensation underneath my skin amplifies a craving for relief.

My acupuncturist stops in the room. I see her reach over and touch my leg, but I don't feel a sensation that mirrors her contact. With focused eyes, she tells me, "Denise, I'll contact your specialist, Dr. Prasad, and let her know what's happening with you."

I say, "It'll pass. I'll be able to walk later, as soon as it passes through. That's how this usually happens." I was hopeful that my acupuncturist would take me in for my treatment. Instead, she hurries off.

I'd shared this sentiment with my specialist before this event. She was the Chief of Internal Medicine and Integrative Oncology at the University of New Mexico. She took me on as a patient because of the complexity of my case. I'd shared my experience regarding these events with her and that I'd been applying specific essential oils, whole-food-based herbal supplements, and qigong, a breathing meditation while holding a yoga posture, to remedy the situation. She said it was impossible for me to survive such things and that it would have to be witnessed and documented to grasp better what I was sharing. Then, she said aloud that I'd run the Integrative Health Studies Program when I was the Director and sole full-time faculty member at Northern New Mexico College. She and Dr. Smith, my acupuncturist, started the Integrative Medicine Program at UNM. Both knew the tenacity and presence of mind required to keep the program moving forward.

I look to my left, eyes expressing my next words, "I can feel them panicking."

Nurse Cristi, my Primary Care Practitioner (PCP), remains by my side and calmly asks everyone except Amber to leave.

Creator, guide me and everyone around me. Spirit guides, angels, and ancestors, I need your help! If it's my time, please let me go peacefully. Now I have to trust and try to relax.

Another wave of sharp pain courses through my body. I hold in a moan. *I don't want anyone to worry.* My body innately undulates, forcing the breath out of my mouth. Then I hear the familiar crackling sound. *Relax. Let it move through. Remain calm. These events are documented in my health history. Allow someone to witness this event. Let someone help.*

I hear Nurse Cristi gasp. She tries to remain calm but frantically interrupts my train of thought, "Are you okay? Are you okay?"

"I'm okay" gets knocked out of my mouth, matching the staccato of my physical movements. Just as suddenly, my body becomes still again, and I feel a wave of relaxation wash over me. "The sharp pains move."

With my left hand, I point to the base of my skull, where the pain feels sharpest. Cristi places her stethoscope near the base of my skull, my occiput, and asks me to stop talking. I think, *Ha! Good luck with that!*

My vision is blurry. I feel weak. I'm afraid to close my eyes.

Two male paramedics arrive at the clinic and begin their assessment of me as another wave of sharp pain overtakes me. I will my body to remain still. Instead, I offer a symphony of cussing.

"156/121," says one of the Paramedics after he takes my blood pressure in the treatment room.

Did I hear that right? How can they say that so calmly? That's too high! And a far cry from the 120/80 norm for a blood pressure reading. I've been a licensed and practicing chiropractic physician for nineteen years. If I saw a number like that from any of my patients, I'd recommend they go to the Emergency Room immediately.

The paramedics want to start an IV. I refuse. They look to Amber. She concurs. Every time I drink water or eat salt for the last five months, I feel an intense burning sensation within my body. Then I pass crystals in my urine. The pain is tremendous.

The mobile pains might be linked to my blood, possibly moving within my lymph vessels or through my fascia. Is this an allergic reaction to something? These events can be triggered when I lift something heavy or my heart pounds, like when I drink caffeine.

How do I explain the events of the past three and a half years to them while I'm in pain and having difficulty expressing myself effectively? They would never believe it anyway. It's hard for me to believe, and I'm experiencing it.

The ones who see this happen firsthand never forget it. Amber has seen this happen too many times. I'm sure she feels just as frustrated, vulnerable, and exhausted as I. Focus.

Another pair of paramedics, one male and one female, pop their heads in and look on while the first two paramedics work together to place ECG leads on my body to monitor my heart's electrical activity. Some of the areas they place the leads on are numb.

A feeling of urgency is slicing through the silence in the room.

Suddenly, I realize the flurry of creative word choices that effortlessly slipped from my lips a few moments ago and probably traveled through every hallway in this Integrative Clinic. *They may have to rename this room Expletive or Obscenity rather than Chi or Serenity.* I apologize to everyone in the room - both sets of paramedics, Nurse Cristi and Amber - for loudly and creatively cussing. Everyone in the room laughs. The tension softens.

Meanwhile, the essential oils Amber dropped on my hands have diffused into my body and are working.

The paramedics want to take me to the hospital. I look at Amber. She and I have had this discussion numerous times. *What can hospital personnel do without using drugs? Then again, I need some answers.*

"How are we going to pay for this?" I say. Amber applied for Medicaid on my behalf in late November 2013 while we were still living in our home in Santa Fe.

That was six months ago. We haven't heard back from anyone yet.

The female paramedic chimes in, and her grin from my previous collection of cussing transforms into a genuine look of concern. She says that tests must be done within a certain time frame to diagnose what all four paramedics witnessed and recorded properly.

The time frame we have is six hours. We have six hours to get accurate information.

I look at my wife.

"Whatever you want to do," she says.

I say, "Let's go."

The paramedics whisk me away.

Chapter 3

On August 3, 2015, Jim Rendon published an article in Time Magazine titled: "How Trauma Can Change Lives - for the Better." He mentions a concept called post-traumatic growth (PG). In this article, Rendon shares that more than half of all people exposed to a traumatic event practice PG and that those who embody PG outnumber people who experience something more well-known, Post-Traumatic Stress Disorder (PTSD) (Breslau, 2001). Traumatic events happen to everyone, it's how we deal with that trauma and how well we release the internalization of it that allow growth. But, Post-traumatic growth is not a new concept. It was first described in 1996 by Richard Tedeschi and Lawrence Calhoun (Tedeschi, 1996), psychologists who did a study. It published its findings about what people report after they have gone through traumatic events. PG indicates that "growth begins from healing trauma." And after that growth, people report becoming "better versions of themselves" (Rendon, 2015).

Simply remain mindful and in the present moment.

Chapter 4

The ambulance doors close.

"We'd like to begin IV fluids with you immediately," says one of the paramedics.

"No," I groan.

My wife had already told them I have life-threatening reactions to meds, and I'd already refused IV fluids while in the doctor's office. Breathe. Trust.

What can be done in a hospital that doesn't involve drugs? Will anyone be able to help me, given this dilemma? Many medical doctors know very little about holistic healing, don't believe in it, are completely against it, or use holistic means as drugs to treat or mask symptoms. *I know the physicians at this particular hospital do a rotation that involves Integrative Medicine. So, I know they have been exposed to the theories of herbal supplements, homeopathic remedies, Traditional Chinese Medicine, and meditation. They'll know how to incorporate them with Western Medicine. I hope my decision to go to the ER is worth the agony of prolonging this experience. If I were at home, I would have continued to apply essential oils until the symptoms resolved as much as possible. The problem is that each event leaves me with residual effects and depleted function of body and mind. Test results can provide more information. I hope they will offer more answers.*

The paramedic attaches leads and runs another ECG. He asks me to resist while he tests arm and leg strength, then repeats the test and writes something down. My eyes follow his pen in an H pattern. He watches my face as I speak. I'm still slurring my words. The paramedic furrows his eyebrows and leans forward. With his hands on my neck, he asks me to swallow. Then sits back and writes something down. I recognize the battery of neurological tests he is doing from my training as a chiropractic physician.

Amber follows behind the ambulance in our blue Subaru Outback.

I notice a grasshopper sitting on my toe and feel the energetic presence of grandpa Manny, who passed away from a stroke when I was a toddler.

As I ponder my mortality, I think of my regrets - not finishing the book I meant to write, not sharing a holographic health perspective more, and withdrawing from countless situations without saying a proper goodbye. *I can't die now! I still have things to do!*

The ambulance rolls up to the hospital.

How are we going to pay for this?

I'm wheeled into the ER. Within moments, the paramedics stop the attending ER doctor, rattle off their findings, and then ask if they should wheel me back immediately for further testing. They begin to unlock the wheels. The attending doctor looks around and asks where my IV is. They say I refused it. The ER doctor pauses and looks at me. Then, he asks me to smile. I smile, but I don't know what it looks like from my point of view. He asks me to speak. I'm able to speak after having applied the essential oils. Then, he asks me to raise my arm. I follow his direction and raise my arm. The doc says no further immediate neurological workup will be done. The paramedics look at each other, stunned. I'm stunned too! I close my eyes briefly to remain calm after hearing this news.

I hope I'll be tested within the next six hours.

One paramedic asks, "Does anyone know what's going on with you?"

I say, "Not yet. I've been trying to get answers for over three and a half years. Nobody's been able to help me. I've used trial and error with holistic means to keep myself on my feet. So far, I've managed to get through these events, but they keep happening more frequently. This is the third time this has happened this week. Nobody's been able to figure out what's causing these events. If we knew the cause, we'd try to remove it!"

He says with eyes wide open, "Well, *something* is going on! Is it some weird fibromyalgia thing? I hope they figure it out. We saw what happened in that office, and the data we captured reflects some of what we saw."

I felt grateful for professional eyewitnesses bearing empirical proof of what I'd been experiencing and describing to disbelieving ears for quite some time.

This domino effect of pain started on October 13th, 2010, after Dr. Ann, my primary care and functional medicine physician, pressed gently on my right ovary during a routine physical exam. That pressure sent a shock wave of pain that bound my tissue from head to toe and was isolated on the right side of my body. I went in for a physical exam to find a way to completely rid my body/mind of a recurring right breast mass.

Dr. Ann, an MD, did several tests, and I'd tried several pharmaceuticals as therapy. I experienced iatrogenic effects from the drugs. In other words, my body could not metabolize the drugs, which worsened my condition.

In 2013, I made an appointment with a new practitioner to establish care with her. The results from the tests she performed and ordered warranted a referral to a specialist. She referred me to Dr. Prasad, the Internal Medicine, and Integrative Oncology Chief at the University of New Mexico.

Dr. Prasad and I shared commonalities as physicians and educators in integrative health. She agreed to take my case. That gave me hope.

I distributed my health history and medical test results to Dr. Prasad while a medical student doing integrative medicine rounds was present. She listened and asked questions. Dr. Prasad explained to the intern that some of my tests were ordered by an MD who practiced Functional Medicine, which focuses on the root causes of disease and offers individualized treatment plans based on physiological markers and tendencies. My specialist took her time listening and documenting the specifics of my case.

Dr. Prasad said that the events I'd described were difficult to believe and that I shouldn't have survived if I had experienced those events and used holistic remedies. I agreed. And, yet, there I was, sitting and talking to her. "There were cumulative after-effects of each event," I said and pointed to my cane. I explained that I understood it was difficult to work with someone unable to take pharmaceuticals. I'd experienced severe allergic reactions to each one I'd tried over the previous four years. Many diagnostic tests require the administration of drugs. I voiced that I wasn't trying to be difficult. I hoped she could help me. She thanked me for acknowledging the difficulty of the situation and said she would do her best to offer me solutions to my conundrum.

Dr. Prasad ordered tests. She said the events I'd described needed empirical tests to know more about my health. I knew from her biography that she was an Ayurvedic physician and a Medical Doctor, and I asked if she could treat me using Ayurveda. She said she couldn't help using Ayurveda in this setting and informed me of a center with Ayurvedic practitioners. Then, she referred me to Dr. Smith for acupuncture and said she was a pain specialist and Doctor of Oriental Medicine (DOM). I agreed to make an appointment with Dr. Smith.

During this event, I was on my way to an appointment with Dr. Smith. Here I am in the ER. Emergency medical personnel are eye-witnessing and obtaining empirical evidence through test results for this event. I'm complying with what Dr. Prasad requested.

I felt vulnerable, which triggered feelings surrounding my experience of childhood traumas. Between the ages of four and eight, I'd been threatened not to tell anyone about the abuses caregivers had generously doled out to me and another girl entrusted in their care. Offering the truth of any situation, especially one that stirs up a tremendous amount of fear and pain, is a vulnerable thing to do. I believe it's best practice to believe and confirm, whether regarding abuse or a serious health condition, to keep the momentum moving in a healthy direction.

As a child, good fortune arrived when my family bought a house and moved to a new location. I was no longer exposed to those abusive caregivers. After the move, I often refused to go to the newly appointed babysitters even though they were a kind family. My trust and boundaries had been breached. Instead, I became a latchkey kid and learned autonomy at a young age.

Amid this health challenge, I effortlessly went into survival mode, isolating myself. I only allowed people I completely trusted to help me. I trusted Dr. Prasad and Dr. Smith. I would comply with their requests if they needed more information to help me.

Almost an hour after arriving at the ER, Amber walks irritated into my room carrying the red and black American Veterinary Chiropractic Association (AVCA) Convention bag I packed earlier that morning.

Amber says, "Are you doing okay? The information booth personnel scoffed when I mentioned I was trying to find my wife. The nurse came out and said you sent her to look for me. I didn't know I had to put my name on a list to come back here."

The automated blood pressure cuff sounds off and gives my arm another squeeze. I look at the reading. 129/89. My blood pressure is slowly normalizing, but it's still higher than it's been lately. It has been uncharacteristically low over the past four or five years.

I say, "I'm glad you found me. I asked the nurse if she could find you in the waiting room because I'd been here a while. I thought you were probably worried. She gave me a disapproving look when I mentioned that you're my wife. Coming out as holistic in this Western Medical world is on par with coming out as gay. I don't understand why living and loving the way my heart sees fit is so offensive," I say.

We shrug, then gaze at each other with appreciation and gratitude for the moment. We silently bask in the presence of each other's company and relax a little.

Chapter 5

Nurses check in regularly. My blood pressure steadily and consistently works its way back into a more normal range. I feel a sensation beneath my skin as if embers from a fire are smoldering. The pain persists. Sometimes it moves from one place to another. My right-sided headache remains. Slowly, my ability to think and physically function returns. I'm able to get up. My movements are slow and deliberate.

A few hours pass. Amber leaves the hospital to go home and let the dogs out.

Quiet isolation and stillness are challenging for me. That's when physical and emotional pain becomes evident. Up until the past three and a half years, I spent my life trying to run from pain, sometimes in very creative ways. I kept myself busy. My best options are to remain aware and discover a way for my body to heal. I feel helpless in an unfamiliar environment amongst people who may or may not understand my holistic health practices. I find peace within stillness when I face unresolved memories and choose the most beneficial pathway for my body, mind, and spirit.

My headache is intense. I close my eyes. It's as if I pull a screen down to play a slideshow of images and feelings I'd tried to forget for decades. A memory flashes to my mind leaving an image of myself as a child overpowered and violated by a caregiver. I feel the urge to run but can't escape.

The seal has been broken, and memories unleashed. Another image surfaces from a few months ago of me steeped in my diluted bright red blood, slumped over the side of the bathtub with Amber pleading, "Please don't die!"

I remember praying from the depths of my soul, requesting God's grace. I prayed for God to take me that night or show me how to heal. Shortly after that prayer, a tingling sensation overcame my body, and physical pain left long enough for me to fall asleep. A few hours later, Amber left for work. I lay on the bed with our two dogs and cats cradling me on all sides. I was surprised to wake up. I repeatedly listened to the song *Carry Me Through* by David Barnes while I sobbed to release the tension and confusion of that week's events.

I bring my attention back to the present moment, in the hospital ER room, and decide to put PG into practice. Knowing that *energy flows where attention goes*, I shift my thoughts to memories I cherish, which brings joy to my heart. I remember the feeling of my heart opening when I found a herd of majestic wild mustangs. When the proud black stallion saw me watching them from the cab of my pickup truck, they animatedly trotted and then galloped away. I feel breathless and exhilarated witnessing their display of athleticism.

Next, I remember the mixed feelings of safety and grit surrounded by the steady, structured beat of house music in a warehouse full of people. Each one of us is engulfed in our outward expressions of ecstatic dance. I remember a magical moment in my classroom while teaching pathophysiology when the mood shifted from confrontation to collaboration between nursing and Integrative Health Studies students. Both groups realized that science and ancient methods shared the common goal of healing. I remembered dancing salsa...

My memories are interrupted by the blood pressure cuff squeezing my arm to capture another reading. I open my eyes. I feel hopeful.

The pharmacist arrives. "I understand you aren't on any medications."

"Correct."

"You are on many supplements."

"I am," I answer.

"Someone took much time and care to enter all of these into your chart."

"Yes, they did," I acknowledge.

"It says here that you are allergic to ibuprofen, dehydroepiandrosterone (DHEA), diazepam, hydrocortisone, naproxen sodium, penicillin, amoxicillin, Novocain, and lidocaine. Anything else?"

"I've stopped trying drugs after having life-threatening reactions to every pharmaceutical medication I've tried over the past five years. I decided to go about healing using holistic methods, and I take full responsibility for that choice," I say with integrity.

"I have that information in my records. Thank you."
The pharmacist leaves the room.

Amber returns. "How are you doing?"

"I'm okay. How are the kids?"

"They're fine. Have they tested you for anything yet?"
She then looks around and hands me contraband, a ham
sandwich, and coconut water.

"Not yet. The nurses pop in regularly to check on me.
They still won't let me have anything to eat or drink. I'm
guessing it's because I couldn't swallow earlier, and they
don't want me to choke." I take a bite of my sandwich.
"The window for accurate test results is closing."

Chapter 6

After the sixth hour in the ER, the resident assigned to my case enters the room. I share my history with him. As he writes notes, he fidgets. He furrows his brow and squints his eyes when he looks at me. He stops writing, cocks his head, and leans on one arm. I continue to tell him what's been happening.

I tell him today's incident was the least severe of the three this week. He tilts his head slightly forward. I see the tension building on his shoulders. He mentions that there is often a transient ischemic attack (TIA) or *warning stroke* before a big one hits. I mention that these events began just after Thanksgiving of 2012 and have been steadily increasing in frequency since that first eight-hour ordeal. I ask him what could cause the sudden onset of severe and unusual symptoms like the ones I've been experiencing over the past several years. He silently looks at me blankly. My experiences were not in any textbooks.

I offered the selected history to the resident. I'm quite sure it was delivered in a difficult-to-understand spray of details. My brain wasn't fully functional at that particular moment.

I continued to say that I'd been striving to maintain balance by eating an organic diet, taking herbal supplements formulated with whole foods, using essential oils, homeopathy, acupuncture, rest, and qigong daily. Also, I'd been a practicing doctor of chiropractic for nineteen years and taught classes in Integrative Health Studies at a college for seven years. In other words, I had practical experience and knowledge regarding using holistic modalities and practices. I didn't see what I was doing as using modalities but rather that it was my lifestyle. I was very animated about this subject, and I was clearly passionate about it.

He said, "Thank you. I want to order a vascular study of your neck, blood tests, and a CT scan with contrast of your brain."

Informed consent allowed me to decline the contrast due to my reactions to meds and agree to the CT scan without contrast, vascular study, and blood tests.

"Okay. Let me speak to my attending physician, and we'll get going on the tests," he said.

He was gone for almost two hours.

Amber had left to feed the dogs and prepare the townhouse for her sister's visit.

When Amber returned, I told her I hoped I would have been released by game time. We needed to let our friends know we wouldn't be there for our first summer league basketball game. We were the players as well as the coaches of the team. I asked Amber to take some pics so they'd see I was okay. I didn't want them to worry.

She took a few pics. I am smiling in them, but I don't look okay.

Around the eighth hour of being in the ER, two more people entered the room, a student and his attending physician.

They wanted to insert a Peripherally Inserted Central Catheter, also known as a PICC line, so they wouldn't have to stick me several times if they needed to draw more blood, insert an IV, or administer meds later. I asked what they would do if I had an adverse reaction to IV fluids. He said it was only a saline solution. I told him that the coating erodes off my tongue and that I feel a severe burning sensation inside my body when I drink water or eat anything salty. That was often followed by spontaneous bruising, bleeding from my gums, passing crystals in my urine, and bloody stool. I had no idea why these symptoms occurred. He was as baffled as I was. He looked at me blankly and said they would give me steroids to counteract the effects of the IV if I had an adverse reaction. Forcing myself to remain calm, I asked what he would do if I had an adverse reaction to steroids.

Amber fidgeted. I was visibly irritated. When she fidgeted, I knew to be quiet. I stopped speaking.

I hoped he was aware of my history and medication reaction. He said they would give me another drug to counteract the first two interventions.

I took in a deep breath and exhaled. At that moment, I accepted the responsibility that informed consent allows me to choose the next steps. I decided not to allow them to insert a PICC line and agreed to get blood tests.

Several tubes of blood were drawn directly from my arm. I was wheeled into imaging for a head CT scan without contrast. The attending physician, a neurologist, decided not to do the vascular study of my neck that I had agreed to allow to be performed. I don't know why.

Soon after my blood pressure reached the much preferred 110/70, compared to the 156/121 measured by paramedics earlier that day in the clinic, Amber's sister arrived from Colorado. Amber met her in the hallway and escorted her into the ER room I'd been assigned. Test results from the five tubes of blood that were drawn revealed slightly low potassium levels. All other blood lab results were within normal limits. The CT scan without contrast also came back within normal limits. I was diagnosed with a Transient Ischemic Attack (TIA), also known as a "warning stroke." I suspected I'd been having TIA's, and it was unnerving to have that diagnosis confirmed. It was particularly unnerving because that was the third "warning stroke" within the same week, and I wasn't any closer to discovering their cause.

My saving grace was that I'd incorporated holistic remedies and lifestyle choices that kept me afloat for the time being. My spirituality was growing. I didn't know why I was still on this planet, but just as everyone has a purpose, I guessed that God decided I had yet to fulfill mine. I remained present, followed my instincts, trusted my research, and nurtured my connection with my spirit guides, ancestors, and angels. I tapped into a well of resilience I didn't know I had. My faith and spirituality were being put into practice by delving into my natural ability to mine benevolent unseen realms for assistance.

I took one step at a time, maintaining faith that I would know where to take the next step. I gained a new perspective with each step I took and the application of each new bit of information.

I was released ten and a half hours after rolling in on a gurney via ambulance earlier that morning. The discharge nurse gave me a stack of papers with information about TIA's and asked me if I understood the information she reviewed with me. I said yes. She said they wanted to give me potassium pills. I thanked her and said I preferred to eat foods rich in potassium instead.

The neurologist told me I should be referred to a neurologist when I see my Primary Care Practitioner again.

I was grateful I got more information and a diagnosis of these repeated events. Most importantly, emergency medical personnel witnessed and recorded this moment for my sanity and the sanity of my wife and specialists. The events I was describing in my health history were confirmed by science.

Amber, her sister, and I left the hospital, papers in hand. Deep gratitude enveloped me as I embraced each intentional step toward another opportunity to live fully. I was surrounded by love and family. I felt fortunate to have faced fears and embraced the day's events as benevolent catalysts of change. I innately healed, unknowingly practicing post-traumatic growth, and pivoted my approach to healing.

Chapter 7

It takes tremendous courage to be honest, and transparent about your life. Many individuals withhold information about the core of their being out of fear of rejection or safety. I believe it's important to be true to who you are. We must remember to be our own best advocates for the choices we make in life at all times.

The 2012 National Institute of Health (NIH) survey demonstrated that one-third of Americans use alternative medicine (Christensen, 2015). According to the data, most people integrated Western medical means with holistic healing to benefit their overall health. Approximately 5% of the population used holistic means as their only path to good health and wellness (Stussman, 2015).

Innovation is key for at least 5% of the population when faced with a healthcare system that touts curing over healing. For innovation to occur, you need a point of stability, so there's a reference point to guide any adjustments you make to the dynamic aspects of your life. That stability is knowing who I am at the core of my being and having the courage to lock myself into that essence. When I settle into my truth, I make lifestyle choices that move me toward wellness and wholeness.

What is the difference between curing and healing? Healing occurs when the body, mind, emotions, and spirit harmonize. It's when an individual's entire system reaches dynamic homeostasis and overall balance. Healing can occur with or without outside intervention. It is something the body does innately. In other words, the body's physiological design is to reach a dynamic state of homeostasis. For example, when you cut your finger, your body sends clotting factors and platelets to stop the bleeding, white blood cells to prevent infection, and remodels damaged tissue. The body does this and more without any direction. Our physiological design also employs this dynamic response to other pathological imbalances within the body. When we work with the body's response toward the direction of better health, we participate in the healing process. We can do this by making beneficial lifestyle choices, such as eating a healthy diet specific to our health presentation and exercising within our body's limits. Healing is a sustainable practice.

While healing occurs from within, curing happens to us from an outside source. Curing aims to eradicate a specific condition completely. The process of curing relies on the process of healing and must regard the body's natural responses to outside influences. For example, an oncologist may treat a diagnosed cancer patient with surgery, chemotherapy, or radiation. To cure a patient of cancer would indicate that it would never recur. The cancer patient's doctor can apply the proper standard of care, and the patient must include healthy lifestyle choices to help their body recover efficiently and effectively.

In essence, healing is a responsible and sustainable dialog. It costs time, energy, focus, and change. The patient and the practitioner are invested in the outcome for the benefit of all. I'd love to see a patient-centered healthcare system that promotes sustainable wellness. True healing.

I realized that healing requires real change.

I believe that hospital personnel missed an opportunity to observe what happens in a healing body without using physiology-altering drugs. They could have witnessed the ability of the body to repair itself with nontoxic substances and minimal input. I employed a sustainable practice for the patient and doctor and the external and internal environment. Why not ask what is working for that patient? There were well-trained healthcare professionals who witnessed and recorded these events.

Why not delve into why someone's body cannot metabolize drugs rather than ignore the patient's lived experience? Why should someone choose between possibly dying of anaphylactic shock or their ailment? There are other options. Let's innovate and collaborate.

Holistic practices often poetically paint the big picture. Western Medicine offers clarity with specificity. If we could work together for the greater good, similar to an ecosystem function, I believe we'd see a wave of true healing on a grand scale.

When we find a way to face and heal trauma, we find a way to laugh again.

The difference between survival and living fully begins with being honest and transparent with yourself. It's the difference between curing and true healing.

DreamWeaving Notebook

Plus (+)

- Resilient
- Courage to speak the truth
- Knowledge of and experience with holistic modalities/practices
- Experience as a chiropractic physician

Delta (△)

- Unknown cause of unusual health condition(s)
- Unable to take pharmaceuticals without severe adverse reactions or allergies
- A daunting task was ahead of me

Holographic Health Assessment - train of thought

- In survival mode - Kidneys - Water Element - must have more courage than fear to survive
- Liver, Spleen, Lung = innovation organs in TCM = Wood, Earth, Metal elements = working
- Fear of unknown - Kidneys - see above - fear
- Unable to metabolize meds - liver and kidneys filter out toxins in the allopathic system - TCM Wood and Water elements
- Need to digest all this info - TCM Earth element

Solutions: listen with an open mind; educate yourself; be transparent; practice what you teach.

The message of hope: the truth shall set us free, and stubbornness can be used for good.

SECTION 2

LEVITY

Lightheartedness & awareness lift consciousness

Chapter 8

A year and a few weeks after my ride to the ER, I experienced another opportunity for growth.

Summer 2015, early one Sunday morning
Cedar Rapids, Iowa

I was in the bathroom preparing the materials for my external castor oil pack. I was going to apply it to painful areas of my body during Amber's DreamWeaving aromatherapy session. When I finished gathering the materials, I stepped out into the hallway and saw a shadow to my right. I turned my head and was surprised to see my uncle standing at the top of the stairs, shoulders squared, eyes forward. I was fully committed to the hallway, wearing only my leopard print skivvies and clutching my hot water bottle like a running back would a football. I streaked three steps across the hallway, flashing uncle Bops a glimpse of my tattoos.

I felt embarrassed at that moment. However, I discovered that transparency offers opportunities to heal. All's well that ends well, yes?

Chapter 9

I learned about applying external castor oil packs from an Ayurvedic physician during the mid and late 1990s. Ayurveda originated in India thousands of years ago and is translated as "the science of life." I sought out that physician for her help with alleviating chronic debilitating menstrual cramps and to learn more about holistic methods of healing. That physician took my health history and checked variations within my pulse, known as pulse diagnosis, to identify imbalances within my organ systems and doshas, which are energetic markers that help identify physiologic, mental, and emotional characteristics. She assessed all of the gathered information and combined it with her knowledge of the five elements of Ayurveda. (Patwardhan, 2022). Then, she formulated a plan in much the same way a Western Medical physician would, except she applied holistic methods rather than prescription drugs or surgery. She prescribed specific herbal remedies, daily external castor oil pack applications, and dietary and lifestyle changes to correct imbalances in my doshas.

I followed her recommendations. Some practices helped alleviate my symptoms, while others or herbal formulas didn't. I stopped incorporating those that didn't help and continued implementing beneficial practices and changes. Making lifestyle changes and applying an external castor oil pack were the most beneficial practices I learned from that Ayurvedic physician. It was life-changing. I continued to research holistic healing modalities experientially. Even though the lifestyle changes improved my health, the original reason for attending the Ayurvedic physician continued to exist and evolve.

In 1998, I first detected a mass in my right breast when I underwent breast cancer screening at the Lesbian Community Cancer Project. At that center, I was not referred for further testing because that small lump had well-defined borders, usually benign. I'd thought about having doctors surgically remove it but decided not to because experts deemed it benign.

Then, in December of 2000, I'd begun to feel uncharacteristically fatigued. I was with a different partner then, Kika, who had found a tender mass in the same spot mentioned above. I'd been training since 1996 in a self-healing practice with a friend whose husband was a well-respected radiologist. I didn't have insurance then, so he offered to do a mammogram at the hospital where he worked. The mammogram and diagnostic ultrasound performed mid-January 2001 revealed a small complex mass. He recommended a biopsy. He explained that the mass could be something that wasn't immediately threatening or fast-growing. Either way, it was a complex mass with irregular borders, possibly malignant.

I'd always been strong-willed and able to support my beliefs with action. I told the radiologist I would like to heal holistically using diet, exercise, and the self-healing practices I was learning. I requested to return in six months for surveillance of the mass. I like to see empirical evidence whenever possible to make well-informed decisions. He said I might not have six months, depending on the biopsy report. I refused the biopsy and reiterated that I would like to see if this could work and promised to call him if I began to feel the mass grow via palpation or if my symptoms worsened. He could see I was firm in my decision, flashed a concerned look, and handed me the films. I made another appointment at the same hospital with the same radiologist and diagnostic ultrasound tech six months after that day. As I drove away from the hospital, the word *malignant* echoed in my mind.

I thought back to my experience with an employer named Karen in 1991 when I was a live-in caregiver for her. She embarked on a holistic healing journey prompted by her diagnosis of malignant breast cancer. My duties included meal preparation, cooking and administration of Chinese herbs and homeopathy, and watching the movie *Pretty Woman* with her. I would also debride the areas of her breast where the tumors were eroding and erupting from the skin, then apply a salve to the exposed tissue. Only her partner and I did that last endeavor.

Karen and her partner, Diane, owned a massage school. Part of my payment was that Diane taught me how to give a professional massage and about essential oils. I was wet behind the ears regarding anything having to do with healing. Since I'm a kinesthetic learner who learns by doing, I was a sponge with all things spiritual and holistic. I required quite a bit of healing for my own seen and unseen wounds. When I was weary or had severe menstrual cramps, I steeped myself in D. Gary Young's essential oil-infused bath gels called *Evening Peace* and *Morning Start*. I met a community devoted to healing and many who regularly raved about receiving regular Network Chiropractic adjustments from Dr. Sue Brown. I didn't know it at the time, but I had been introduced to the work of people that would have a profound impact on my work and dramatically change the course of my life from that moment on. I couldn't deny the courage and support I witnessed during the three months I was a caregiver living in Karen and Diane's home. That experience defies words.

I'd met another woman, Bea, who'd healed from breast cancer using holistic methods. I invited her to speak at the chiropractic college I was attending. I remember the scene of her sharing her story in one of the lecture halls as if it was yesterday.

I truly believed then, as I do now, that if the body could put something in place, the body could also remove it. I thought back to the anatomy lab in chiropractic college when we dissected cadavers. What struck me most was how the details differed slightly for each person depending on their health picture and lifestyle choices. In other words, the body was extremely adaptable and resilient.

In 2001, I had six months to put my beliefs to the test. I meditated, then engaged mentors and teachers in conversations. I took the advice to heart and practiced the offered suggestions from those I sought guidance from. That was the respectful thing to do. I drank at least ten glasses of water daily and got chiropractic adjustments from Dr. Sue Brown about twice a month. I eliminated refined sugar from my diet and began the first wave of daily self-healing practices - intestine movements to decongest *qi*, loosely translated as energy, and keep my organs pliable. I practiced qigong, a breathing meditation while holding a yoga posture to strengthen my core, to clarify, increase, and move qi. I did chest breathing for twenty minutes daily to move lymph and help remove emotional blocks. Additionally, I incorporated a healthy diet and exercise. The second wave of training included intestine movements, chest breathing, and qigong. I also did bowing training, like burpees without kicking your feet out, five-hundred times daily for clarity of body, to gain better balance, and to renew my commitment to my life's purpose. The only way to know if what I was doing would help improve my health was to try it. I practiced religiously.

When I arrived at my follow-up appointment in July 2001, my radiologist looked relieved to see me. I didn't know what results to expect. The mammogram was done. The results showed that both breasts were completely clear. All of us were shocked! He looked at me, then back at the film. He compared films and showed them to the ultrasound tech. Then he said, "Those don't even look like the same breasts." I assured him they were mine in both films. All of us laughed off the tension. He returned the original set of films to me and kept the second set. I sang all the way home during that car ride. This time, during my drive home, the only thing that echoed in my mind was the feeling of collaborative relief and laughter.

That experience opened my eyes to the need to have more things I love daily. One of my aunts mentioned that we had Native blood, but she didn't give me more details. I was naturally drawn to all things Indigenous, so I consciously continued frequenting drumming circles and sweat lodges. There was a notice on Dr. Sue Brown's bulletin board regarding a drumming circle being held at Spirits Whisper Acres, a holistic horse ranch owned and operated by Virginia Litza. I brought my Taos drum to it. Virginia and I became immediate friends.

Next, I began donating my time to the ranch once or twice a month. I donated chiropractic adjustments or bodywork on people and animals, mucked out stalls, and fed and groomed horses. I felt great to support a business I believed in so it could flourish.

Then, several events and health challenges prompted our move to New Mexico.

One day while at practice for flag football, I injured my back. I couldn't get up or move without excruciating pain. I didn't want to go to the hospital. My teammates brought one of my Lloyd portable chiropractic tables to the field and carried me away on it as if it were a gurney.

Kika contacted a friend who contacted Master Yoon, one of the Korean teachers who oversaw those I'd studied qigong with. Master Yoon came to Kika's and my apartment and gave me an hour and a half acupuncture treatment. I began to relax. I felt much better but remained recumbent and flat and had difficulty standing or walking. When we asked him how much I owed him, he replied, "Share your energy with the world." I was grateful for his generosity and wealth of knowledge.

I rested that night, and the next day I started visualizing myself practicing qigong to support the work Master Yoon had done until I could physically perform the practice.

A few days later, while recovering from my injury, Kika called me from work and told me to turn on the tv. It was on the morning on September 11, 2001. I felt disbelief and shock when I saw footage of planes crashing into the sides of the twin towers of the World Trade Center. It was a surreal experience. I thought of all of the people in those buildings and planes. I watched footage of people jumping from windows and running down streets covered in soot and debris. Brave firefighters were moving opposite the panicked and frightened citizens, attempting to treat the wounded and save as many people as possible. It was a day I'll always remember. It was a tragic day that eventually brought about the compassion and unification of the citizens of the United States of America.

I felt helpless regarding the images I saw on the tv while I healed. Those events inspired me to reflect on what I could rather than what I couldn't do. It inspired me to heal and move toward realizing my dreams.

I made a resolve to honor Master Yoon's request. That required me to focus on my happiness. Then, I sat quietly with my thoughts and realized my heart desired to live in the mountains and to be near horses. I also wanted to share what I'd learned regarding self-care exercises that incorporated body/mind/emotion/spirit. These exercises were affordable because their practice only costs time, energy, and focus once learned. I planned to begin teaching and asked Kika what she thought about moving. She was open to it. We aimed to have land and a safe, inclusive space for people to visit and heal. There would be small huts as accommodations representing different parts of the world. There would be horses for interactive healing seminars and training areas for elite athletes. We booked a reconnaissance vacation to northern New Mexico.

I carefully and slowly practiced qigong and the form of tai chi from previous Korean teachers. I was able to walk without a cane after ten days.

However, I had returned to the same dietary and lifestyle habits I'd adopted before the mass was detected. Gradually, I felt pain occupying the area where the original mass had been. In time, I palpated my right breast and felt the unwanted lump underneath my fingertips. It was growing noticeably larger and more painful faster than the one detected earlier that year. How could that happen? It was supposed to be gone. Wasn't I cured? I meditated for guidance and reinstated a healing regimen that included good nutrition, a steady diet of qigong, breathing exercises, doing what I love, journalling, and meditation.

Part of doing what I loved included spending time around horses and kind, compassionate people. I continued volunteering at Spirits Whisper Acres, and when I mentioned my dilemma to Virginia, she said, "Have you ever tried essential oils?" I told her I had, but I didn't notice much difference when I tried them. She asked if they were good quality. I didn't know and said I'd tried them twice. Once when I worked at a crystal store during my last year of undergrad at Northern Illinois University and then when I'd worked as a caregiver for Karen and Diane in 1991. She told me that quality matters.

Virginia told me that good quality essential oils required pure growing conditions and the knowledge of how to grow, harvest, extract, and store the oil to obtain the most beneficial healing properties. The purity of the water source, soil, altitude, air quality, harvest times, and how the plants are harvested affect quality. Then, the amount of pressure and time allocated during the distilling process had to be optimal to yield the proper chemistry. A nonreactive type of material the cooker is made of was necessary too. One didn't want to make such a huge effort to tend to high-quality, pesticide and insecticide-free plants and then cook them in something that would leach aluminum, copper, or lead into the oil.

Virginia had my attention. All of the things she said made sense to me. I'd heard and read the same concepts concerning food, tea, and herbal supplements as a chiropractic assistant and as Karen's live-in caregiver. I continued to listen.

She went on to say that some oils, most citrus oils, were cold-pressed rather than distilled. And it was best for that process to be done without chemicals to avoid contaminating the final product with anything more than what nature intended.

They also needed to be bottled in glass or alabaster, then stored properly in a cool, dry place that didn't get direct sunlight. Increased heat or the introduction of moisture could alter the chemistry of the carefully grown and distilled or pressed oil.

Virginia asked if I'd be willing to receive a Raindrop Technique®, which was the layering of a specific set of essential oils in a specific order. She said it was a unique practice intended to rejuvenate the body and mind and based on methods used for centuries, some of which were Indigenous practices.

I'd been to Spirits Whisper Acres for a women's sweat lodge the week prior. A sweat lodge could be described as an Indigenous practice where a safe and sacred space allows the participants a place of introspection, meditation, and communion with one another and our ancestors. All are encouraged to reconnect with the earth and renew social and cultural bonds.

I didn't think the oils would help my predicament, but I was open to trying them. I received my first Raindrop Technique® from a registered nurse, Virginia's sister. It was an intense experience.

It only took two weeks for the aggressive right breast mass to subside in size and pain after adding the sweat lodge and essential oils to the same rigorous healing discipline I'd employed. The difference between two weeks versus six months in decreasing the mass size, pain, and fatigue had my attention. I still wasn't convinced that essential oils worked, but now they were back on my radar.

Under Virginia's guidance, I gave my first Raindrop Technique® to a horse that had West Nile Virus. I also worked with a squirrel, an owl, chickens, horses, dogs, and cats with varied health issues. One day, I watched Virginia descend upon and gently pick up an injured hawk sitting at the far end of one of the pastures. She rushed past me toward the house at a fast-paced walk, telling me that I would adjust the hawk. I followed her wide-eyed, shaking my head at her confidence in me. I gave a non-force chiropractic adjustment to that hawk, as I'd learned in Dr. Sue Brown's seminars. Then, Virginia guided me on using the oils safely and effectively, diluting them with carrier oils like coconut or some other fat-based substance rather than water.

I learned and grew my skills, then donated them.

Then, an opportunity arose for Kika and me to move to Northern New Mexico. We decided to go. Preparations were made. I informed my patients of the planned move that would take place in three months and referred them to several other practitioners.

I lived at Spirits Whisper Acres for a month before the move to learn more about holistic animal care firsthand. I also wanted to share the self-care knowledge I'd cultivated with others.

I'd witnessed the effects of the relational use of different healing modalities and practices. I'd observed that the benefits were spotty when modalities weren't designed to work synergistically. But, the results were exponentially beneficial when corresponding modalities were properly applied.

Somehow, the breast masses remained at bay.

Virginia and I did a seminar together that incorporated interaction with the horses. She and I became best friends. Virginia had a commanding presence, a gentle soul, and a kind heart. People were often intimidated by her strength of conviction and direct expression. I was drawn to that kind of truth speak. I was drawn to authenticity in action. She often told me I was the only person to stand up to her. And she was the only person who told me exactly what she thought. We earned mutual respect for one another with a strong work ethic, a penchant for holistic healing, and the courage to step in authenticity.

That experience prompted the pursuit of happiness and the revival of things that I love in my life. Kika and I moved from Chicago to New Mexico in July of 2003 with a gift from Virginia, a Staffordshire Terrier we named Ty-chi, and a lot of essential oils.

While living in New Mexico, my breast imaging adventures continued.

The mass waxed and waned. Painful growth of the mass was usually preceded by or accompanied by symptoms of the presence of debilitating back pain. I used essential oils as needed and complemented the oils with a self-care regime that consisted of a healthy diet, meditation, external castor oil packs, and qigong. My physician referred me for thermograms to keep an eye on the breast mass and possibly detect any major changes that might be of greater concern.

My doctor referred me to Dr. Janet Green, a nationally-respected MD, for a thermogram. A thermogram is a noninvasive test that detects heat signatures beneath the skin's surface. Meeting Dr. Green for the first time was a thought-provoking experience.

It began with paperwork.

Dr. Green took my completed history forms and asked me to follow her into her office so she could read them before doing the thermogram. I must have been in her office for an hour, expanding on my writing. She looked up from my paperwork at me, raised her eyebrows, and took in a deep breath.

She directed me to the exam room. Then, I undressed from the waist up, holding my arms over my head, so my dynamic duo could cool down to room temperature, which is required for this evaluation. Then, she did the painless, non-touch thermogram and asked me to wait while she assessed the results. I dressed and waited. Then, I waited some more.

Forty-five minutes later, Dr. Green returned with an astonished look on her face. She entered the room and asserted that she thought I'd had cancer. The doctor then proceeded to show the identifying markers of why she believed that I'd somehow managed to heal. I had focused on strengthening my overall health, especially my immune system. I changed my diet and lifestyle to eliminate toxins and support a healthy environment in my cells. She shared that she traveled the nation and had yet to find someone who approached anything like this holistically and lived. I had met one woman who had healed and witnessed one woman whose health declined rapidly before my eyes. My doctor and I shared some heartfelt sentiments.

I said we'd never know what the cell histology was because I'd refused biopsies, and pathology tests of tissue samples were Western Medicine's only confirmation of a cancer diagnosis.

I shared the self-healing exercises I'd done for the first recovery from the right breast mass. Then, I shared that the mass had returned with a vengeance after I'd returned to some unhealthy habits. My best friend, Virginia, reintroduced me to therapeutic-grade essential oils. When I added those to what I'd learned from the Korean masters I'd studied with, the mass became smaller within two weeks versus six months. There seemed to be an exponential effect when combining methods in a balanced way.

Dr. Green was a skeptic when I walked into her office. But, when she saw evidence that corroborated my health history, she became one of my best advocates.

Almost a year later, in 2009, Amber and I went to breakfast at *Pasqual's* in downtown Santa Fe. We overheard the conversation of several women while sitting at the community table. They had all come from out of town to see a friend named Janet, who was close to passing away. They reminisced about the time spent with her and shared that she would be missed as a friend and colleague. I soon realized the person they were speaking so highly of was my doctor.

It's disheartening when one of your physicians dies of the disease I suspected I was also experiencing. It was disturbing going to a new thermographer for that reason in 2010. Losing a physician that believes you and shares a common experience is like losing a piece of yourself. It also shines a spotlight on thoughts of your mortality.

On my forty-second birthday, October 19, 2010, Amber took the day off to celebrate together and drive me to scheduled tests Dr. Ann had recommended. We drove forty-five minutes from Santa Fe to Albuquerque, New Mexico. I had difficulty sitting still for that time due to my tremendous pain.

The first stop was to meet my new thermographer, who had a great amount of respect for Dr. Green. The song *Don't Stop Believing* by Journey played in the waiting room as Amber and I entered the office. I was called to the back, where this new thermographer studied my two previous thermograms. She was surprised that Dr. Green gave me a TH4+ rating, indicating that Dr. Green was convinced I had a history of cancer. This thermographer tested me and said she'd review the imaging studies in depth. Then, she'd send her findings to Dr. Ann in Santa Fe.

Amber and I left that doctor's office and stopped for lunch. We had several hours to spend together before the next test, so we detoured to take in the sights at Cochiti Lake.

That day's next test was performed at an imaging center in Santa Fe. The tech indicated she needed to use the transvaginal ultrasound transducer. I opened my eyes wide and said, "Oh, Towanda!" She tried not to laugh - both of us cracked up. I relaxed. During the test, I could communicate to the ultrasound tech exactly where I felt the major problem existed, guided by my sensations. "There! Not so much there. Yes, there! Ugh!" Pain sucked the blood out of my face while the transducer pulsed ultrasonic waves toward my right ovary. The tech's eyes widened, and her muscles tensed. I knew something wasn't quite right when she said she would immediately get the results to my doctor and ran out of the room.

I was confused at how quickly my state of health changed after seeing a doctor for a routine physical exam. I'd gone to check my overall health and find a way to stop the breast mass from returning or eliminate it for good. Instead, something else was uncovered or discovered, and it brought with it a world of hurt.

I was scared. Everybody around me was panicking, including me. I told Amber I wanted to get a banana split for my birthday before I found out I needed to completely eliminate refined sugar from my diet if whatever was triggering so much pain in my right ovarian region appeared malignant.

When we arrived home after the banana split, we barely put our keys down on the kitchen counter when the phone rang. The sound of the ring stirred an ominous feeling inside my gut. It was only an hour after leaving the imaging facility. I answered the phone, and my feeling was confirmed, it was the imaging center. They wanted me to schedule a biopsy immediately and said my MD would call me to schedule an appointment to see her first thing in the morning.

The shock hadn't hit yet. It took a few days for me to digest a serious event or emergency. I tended to take care of whatever I needed, then expressed appropriate emotion three days later.

But, at that moment, I appeared calm. I told Amber I was glad we went for a banana split. Then the phone rang again. It was my Integrative Medicine MD. She, herself, called me. She said she would like me to come in first thing in the morning and then made the appointment.

October 20, 2010
Santa Fe, New Mexico

I was sitting at the kitchen table Amber's parents had given us as a wedding gift a little over a year ago. This beautiful wooden table and chairs were often a meeting place to nourish ourselves, our bodies, and our souls. We made a lot of important decisions at that table together. Amber and I sat facing one another. I kept shifting from side to side and couldn't get comfortable. The pain was intense. I felt fatigued and could barely hold myself up.

I told her I was considering having surgery to remove my ovary. I didn't know if I was strong enough to survive it. A few days ago, I'd felt so weak I couldn't lift my cell phone.

After a long pause, Amber said she'd support my decision. Then asked why I would consider such a thing because it didn't align with who I was. She reiterated that

I didn't respond well to drugs. She, too, didn't think my body was strong enough to survive surgery or a biopsy.

The conversation triggered a memory of me talking to my *Abuelita* on the landline while I was in my office at Northern New Mexico College. I told her how excited I was about Amber and me buying our 1,800 square foot three bedrooms, two-bathroom house in Santa Fe. Abuelita paused, then said she had something to tell me. Suddenly, Shannon, a friend and coworker, alerted me to a bomb threat at the college and said everyone in the building had to evacuate. I let Abuelita know what was going on. I hung up the phone, then evacuated the building.

Even though I wasn't supposed to use a cell phone outside while we were waiting for the all-clear, I wanted to finish my discussion with Abuelita. I called her back. She told me she was going to Los Angeles to see an oncologist about her health. If they found cancer again, she wanted to let it take its course rather than go through more rounds of chemo and radiation.

She had beaten lymphoma going the Western Medical route and went in for PET scans every six months to look for recurring "hot spots" since then. She lost all her hair during that battle and bought a red wig at her husband's suggestion. She looked fabulous in that wig. It was playful, feisty, bright, and energetic. It matched her personality and made her look ten years younger than she was.

Our second conversation was short because she was going to play duplicate bridge with her friends before leaving for Los Angeles. She needed extra time to get there because she was using a walker to get around following a recently failed spine surgery. Not much could stop this woman. I told her I would call her the following day, and we hung up.

The next day, she said the doctor found two masses. One was where her ovary used to be. Something had grown back in its place even though she'd had it surgically removed. The other mass was located in her stomach. Her doctor did biopsies on both masses, and she said she was in so much pain that she didn't know how long she would be able to remain on the phone. She was staying with her youngest daughter, Cielo, and visiting with one of her sisters when I called. A few minutes into our conversation, she said something was wrong and was in tremendous pain. She and I abruptly hung up so family members could take her to the ER. That was the last time I heard her beautiful Salvadoran accent.

Abuelita went to the ER. Within twenty-four hours of the biopsies, cancer infiltrated her chest cavity. There was no evidence of cancer in her chest cavity before the biopsies.

She passed away eight days later at approximately 1:30 am in her ICU room. Amber, Cielo, and I sat at her bedside, drinking whiskey from a jelly jar. We were telling each other what we needed to do to live authentic lives from here on out when we noticed the "death rattle" had stopped, and the room was quiet. I'd promised myself I would share DreamWeaving holographic health and sent up a prayer of gratitude to have had this amazing woman in my life. It was an honor to sit in her presence on her last day on Earth.

I miss my *Abuelita,* yet I still feel her presence and spirit whenever I request her counsel. I love knowing her DNA is embedded in every cell of my body. Her name was Esperanza. Hope.

Chapter 10

The exercise below is an example of Kokology, derived from the Japanese word *Kokoro,* which means "mind" or "spirit." It is a fun and unique approach developed by Tadahiko Nagao and Isamu Saito to help reveal psychological aspects of yourself via hypothetical situations (Dunn, 2000).

Kokology is a holographic personality test for the mind or spirit of a person.

"Imagine yourself walking through a desert...and you see a cube. How big is the cube? What material is the cube made out of? How far is the cube from the ground?

Somewhere near the cube, imagine a ladder. Where is it in relation to the cube? What is the ladder made out of?

Picture a horse next to the cube and ladder. Is it wearing anything? What is the horse doing?

Now, imagine flowers somewhere in the scene. How many are there? How far away are they from the cube?

Lastly, there's a storm starting. How close is it to the cube, ladder, horse, and flowers?

The size of the cube is the size of your ego. The transparency of the cube shows how open you are with people. The closer it is to the ground, the more grounded you are.

The distance between the ladder and the cube shows how close you are to your friends. If the ladder is leaning against the cube, your friends can lean on you for support. The sturdier the material, the stronger your bonds are with people.

The horse being tied up or saddled means you like more control in a relationship. The wilder the horse, the wilder you like your relationships.

The more flowers you picture, the more kids you want. The closer the flowers are to the cube, the more you think about kids.

The storm represents stress. The closer and more threatening the storm is, the more stressed you are." (Pugachevsky, 2014)

It's essential to understand who you are at the core of your being, whether you use kokology to help determine that or some other means. I like kokology because it helps you use the symbology of the concept that form follows function to discover how you feel about different aspects of your life. It also gives a basic understanding of how you relate to others and how every choice holds a metaphor of meaning within it. When we encounter meaningful choices that encompass something we are passionate about, we are drawn to inspired action. When action is inspired rather than forced, we often go to places and do things that lead us to connect with people we can have authentic interactions. Daily authentic interactions leave us feeling satisfaction at the depth of our souls.

Chapter 11

We inherit all aspects of DNA from our ancestors, the good, the challenging, and the bold. This is true of me inheriting the gumption to move to a distant home, just like my Abuelita made a solo move from El Salvador to Chicago at age twenty-one. Kika and I drummed up a lot of courage and faith to move ourselves and our newly inherited dog, Ty-chi, from Chicago to northern New Mexico in a ten-foot U-haul. I can't imagine the amount of courage and gumption it took for Abuelita to move on a work visa to a different country and had to learn English simultaneously.

Santa Fe had always drawn me. Perhaps it was because it was my mom's favorite city or because my great grandparents, Victor and Margarita Vera, once called The City Different their home. Perhaps it was because Diane took me on a healing journey to Ojo Caliente Mineral Springs with money Karen left to her after her passing. I felt as if I'd fallen in love with New Mexico before I visited for the first time. The essence of that state lived in my soul.

Northern New Mexico truly is enchanting and breathtaking. Vibrant communities exude beauty and unspoken resilience. Every expression is heartfelt. And healthy respect is required at all times.

I had every intention of living the last days of my life there. It felt like home. Northern New Mexico was a place and community that had tested my mettle. I had to make difficult choices that involved much letting go. Those choices helped unveil where I stand today. The State of Enchantment taught me that being home meant keeping my wits about me and residing in the present moment, no matter where I was or who I was with.

Chapter 12

October 20, 2010
Santa Fe, NM

Sitting at our wooden kitchen table with Amber.

After a short silence, I say, "You're right. It's my nature to do this holistically. I'm going to refuse the biopsy. I don't think I'm strong enough to fight off any possible seeding once a hole gets poked into a nicely walled-off mass. Abuelita passed away eight days after her biopsies. I can't help but wonder if she and I have similar health tendencies through our DNA. Honey, this mass has a blood supply. I'm so scared! If they find it malignant ovarian cancer, I have about a 5% chance of surviving, and that's with Western medical treatment. I'll get the medical tests my body can tolerate and go the holistic route for treatment."

"I love you," Amber says.

I add, "I also think we need to be careful about whom we share information with and who enters our home. I don't want someone else's fears to taint my understanding of who I am."

"Agreed," Amber nods in confirmation.

Chapter 13

Journal entries

Denise
10/21/10

"Be" who you are. That's my motto these days and every day from here on "out." :) Today has been quite a day. I did four rounds of two full capsules of essential oils down the hatch. Ack! This cleansing, correcting process sucks!

T-low and Danielle came to visit at 2:30 pm. I had fallen asleep for a couple of hours and could barely stand when I went to answer the door. T-low had to take my arm to help me to the bathroom. When I finally went, the color started to return to my face.

I need to stand by my resolve. My body may be deflating a bit, but the fire in my heart and soul is being stoked with encouragement and support from our friends and family.

I'm so fortunate to be married to a beautiful woman who accepts me for who I am! Oh, happy day!

Denise
10/22/10
8:24am

The body's wisdom far exceeds the amount of knowledge any man or woman can carry.

10:19 am

Yesterday was rough with physical purging. Today is torture with the mental and emotional stuff. All I can do right now is sit in a chair in the middle of the room and cry. I don't want to waste my time with a pity party, but I need to cry.

Denise
10/23/10
2:17am

* I think I've discovered the key piece to DreamWeaving Technique. Identify the correlation of the holographic personality of the individual with the holographic presentation of their health imbalance.*

I tried using oils as chemotherapeutic agents - only made it four "rounds." That was a mistake. The next day, I had less pain in the morning, but my body was so tired that I couldn't sustain the changes. By the end of the day, I was worse off than before I did the oiling. It made sense to me cognitively but didn't pan out with my experience. There must be a way for healing to be sustainable. I'll try again.

All my symptoms are on the right side of my body. I have been overdoing things and letting my ego dictate doing way too much. This points to an abundance of yang, too much activity of my male aspect, "doing" too much, and left brain dominance.

My symptoms match the lack of balance in my actions.

7:39 am

I was applying Western Medical techniques with holistic healing modalities.

I need to dance with this predicament rather than attack it. My cells are attacking me in a very destructive way. I need to find some way to divert the energy going into destructive tendencies into something useful.

There is a Native American parable that involves wolves - one mean and one kind wolf. We all have both aspects, or "wolves," within our persona. The one that survives is the one we feed. In *The Joy of Stress*, Loretta LaRoche says, "You fed it, it's yours." It's time to feed my healthy tendencies and dreams.

11:02 pm

We have turned a corner. The key is remaining calm in the face of something or someone that appears to be a bigger or stronger opponent. I must remain diligent.

Amber
10/23/10

List of initial ideas for oils to use in hands-on DreamWeaver Aromatherapy Application for Denise:

* Elemi - sesquiterpenes, anti-depressant, inflammation of breast and uterus
* Sandalwood - sesquiterpenes, anti-depressant, calming, removing negative programming from cells, pineal gland, balance emotions
* Balancing blend - Spruce, Rosewood, Blue tansy, Frankincense
* Endocrine balance blend - Spearmint - burns fat & toxins; geranium - liver, kidney function; Myrtle - thyroid; Nutmeg - adrenal glands, energy; German chamomile - open liver, increase liver function
* Palo Santo - anti-tumoral

Wood element/Yin
liver
parasympathetic nervous system - Lemongrass (regulates), Marjoram (increases the tone of), Calming blend, Balancing blend

Today we went to qigong, and it was so helpful. I felt so much better afterward.

I gave Denise a hands-on Aromatherapy Application, which helped her turn a corner, which is awesome! I feel so relieved and thankful that she feels better. It's been so awful to see her in so much pain. Thank Goddess, she's feeling better. It makes me happy to know I helped her. Now we need to stay on it. The essential oil order came at the right time. Continue to have fun :) I need to work out every day - this is the perfect time to eat healthily and get the body, mind, emotion, and spirit the healthiest possible!

The time and knowledge Virginia and I shared with one another started a domino effect and returned what was given in more ways than I could ever have imagined. When two people passionate about what they do combine resources and encourage one another to continue to live with authenticity, it's the difference between using two legs to stand on versus using them to move forward. Momentum is created.

A year prior, Virginia flew me to her holistic horse ranch to teach my perspective of healing. She also flew Amber so she could be tech support for the weekend class. Virginia took care of finding the participants, payment, transportation, and lodging for myself and Amber on more than one occasion.

While Amber took care of the tech end of the weekend seminar, she learned the content of the class. She learned the process of observing the holographic personality of an individual and how to choose essential oils that benefit the individual's core health and behavioral characteristics. Amber used that weekend experience and four books to give me a hands-on Aromatherapy Application a year later.

That hands-on approach incorporates the relationship between the body's organ systems and traditional healing systems thousands of years old. The synergism of both systems promoted efficiency and effectiveness for my healing. Given that these concepts are based on natural law, it's reasonable to conclude that this collaboration of detailed information and wisdom could benefit others.

Chapter 14

Summer 2015, early Sunday morning
Cedar Rapids, Iowa

I bounded from the hallway into the bedroom, where Amber rested on the bed. She gave me a curious look. My face was pale.

I told her my uncle was standing at the top of the stairs while I streaked across the hallway clutching the hot water bottle underneath my arm. Her eyes widened. Both of us silently took in those events. Suddenly, we heard uproarious laughter from my aunt and uncle downstairs in the kitchen.

That's when I realized this was a memorable moment for all involved.

Amber looked at my expression and hesitantly laughed.

I felt embarrassed about the condition of my body, mainly that I'd gained weight. I realized I had a choice to make, face or ignore my current condition.

I felt vulnerable. Facing my feelings required me to recall unpleasant memories of the confusing events of the previous years. I was stripped down to the basics of whom I was. My job or title, income, or appearance no longer define me. I chose to see the humor in the situation rather than identify as a victim. I decided to remain present. I didn't understand how or why the series of events occurred. I still didn't know what caused a decline in health to that point. There were many unanswered questions. I had to remain present and pivot my perspective. What could I do at that moment to move forward?

I placed the external castor oil pack over the area I'd felt the most pain. Then, Amber expertly administered essential oils to my back. She'd done this every week for about a year. I thought about the first one she'd done back in October 2010. A lot went into developing this essential oil technique. Virginia taught me how important essential oils are and how quality affects results. Listening to other physicians taught me new concepts, practices, and ideas. There was power in forming meaningful relationships with others. Integrating information I'd learned from other doctors and holistic practitioners combined with knowledge and willingness to apply it with a collaborative and synergistic perspective brought more information and results. Much went into the development of this essential oil technique and application. Every step required me to remain present and choose a healthy direction. I chose to be present at that moment. It was worth it. The pain was decreasing, and the scent of layered essential oils from my skin filling the room was exquisite.

When Amber and I went downstairs, we all laughed, recounting the events as we sat around Uncle Bops and

Aunt Ahma's kitchen table. Each perspective offered a different vantage point and greater levity. Ahma said she was surprised something like that didn't happen sooner. They'd welcomed the two of us, our dog and cat, into their home weeks ago.

Then, Bops left our gathering and went upstairs.

When he returned to the kitchen, he was wearing his King Kong boxer shorts with the mouth yawning wide open at the crotch region over another pair of shorts. He turned around so we could see *Rrrooaarr* written across the back of his shorts. Compassion and laughter filled the kitchen.

The parting gift I got from that memorable moment was the nickname leopard pants. It still makes me grin, cheek to cheek.

DreamWeaving Notebook

Plus (+)

- Nourished by family - blood and chosen
- All in - I put my heart into everything I did
- Remained calm amidst adversity
- Strong-willed

Delta (△)

- Unknown cause of illness
- Difficulty dealing with loss
- Needed acceptance of circumstances, including body issues and health events

DreamWeaving Assessment - train of thought

- Accept things I cannot change or control
- My family and friends are supportive
- Have the courage to try and learn from all experiences
- Gratitude comes with awareness of the gifts of that moment
- Let go of ego and accept help
- Worth has to do with who I am innately
- Keep going - keep getting up - keep assessing - one step at a time

Solution: For best results, learn from all experiences and remain in the present moment.

The message of hope: seeing the lighter side of everything heals a world of woes.

SECTION 3

AND

Connectivity allows synergistic flow

Chapter 15

October 4, 2015
Tiffin, IA

As I walked into the room, Amber said, "That's the best $300 we've ever spent."

I have a quizzical look on my face. She's sitting on a $300 couch watching a $300 TV perched on a $300 TV stand, all of which were unsolicited gifts over the previous three weeks.

"What do you mean?" I ask.

Amber responds, "That Akashic Record reading from Dr. Linda Howe."

I grinned. It's true. I add, "That was truly a gift in every aspect of our lives. Thank you! I'm amazed how one courageous decision that feels right can alter the direction of the lives involved. Here we are, living in Iowa. It took a lot of focus, consistency, and work.

"Remember when we started dating? You didn't believe in any of this woo-woo stuff. A surprising and consistent amount of follow-through goes into holistic healing."

Chapter 16

January 2008
Hernandez, New Mexico

I looked outside. There was Buddy, the nickname I gave the dog who often jumped the fence to hang out and play with my brindle Pitt Bull, Ty-chi. She was a gift from Virginia the day Kika and I left to move to New Mexico. Kika and I were together for seven years. She moved back to Chicago to be with her family after we broke up in 2007. Ty-chi and I remained in Hernandez, New Mexico.

Many individuals I'd met in New Mexico became my extended family.

During this visit, Buddy was standing on the walkway by the water well, looking dazed toward the house I was renting. He wasn't frolicking with Ty-chi as usual.

"What's he doing?" I asked my roommate.

"I don't know," she said.

Buddy jumped the fence and showed up in the yard one day. Ty-chi enjoyed playing with him; if my dog could trust him, I knew I could trust him. The question was, did he trust me? Naturally, I went outside to see how he was doing and immediately noticed blood pulsating out one of his front legs. I looked through the wrought iron-gated front doorway and noticed a pool of bright red blood on the walkway. It matched the stone facade of the adobe house and the two-tiered well that Buddy was standing between.

My roommate was a nurse. She and I knew that anytime blood pulsates and squirts out of an open wound, it indicates a severed artery. Buddy could bleed out if we didn't do something fast. My roommate asked what I needed and hurried inside the house to retrieve supplies while I cautiously approached Buddy. Ty-chi stood nearby with her brow furrowed, glancing from Buddy to me and back to Buddy again. My roommate returned with supplies.

I applied some ointment onto a sterile gauze pad and added drops of Myrrh and Helichrysum to the ointment. Then, I pressed a couple of layers of ointment-laced gauze on the wound to help stop the bleeding. I bandaged and taped the gauze pads to his leg so he could at least make it home, wherever that was.

I gently adjusted Buddy using non- and low-force chiropractic techniques so his nervous system would be free of interference, allowing his body to rebalance and heal itself more quickly. Buddy instinctively knew when the series of adjustments were done, then turned toward the four-foot-tall cinder block fence and jumped over it. I could see the evidence of our care for him as he ran through the neighbor's yard.

I went inside. My roommate turned to me and said, "I think you got your answer."

Just before Buddy jumped into the yard that day, my roommate and I had been discussing the pros and cons of my going through an animal chiropractic program at Parker University in Dallas, Texas. I'd also been discussing the possibility with Amber, whom I'd been dating for a few months.

Amber and I should have known we would have to put out some fires. The first time we met was at *dyke movie night* on the outskirts of Taos. Kika and I went at the invitation of one of the fire chiefs I'd met during a three-day structural fire fighting mini-academy held in Red River, New Mexico. When Kika and I arrived at the house, I was amazed to see so many gay women at this event. The house was nestled in a small town, and we were given descriptive directions that told us to go past the tree with the colossal knot and turn left on the gravel road by the black and white herd of cows.

There were gay women of all ages in this welcoming New Mexican home. Conversations ranged from sharing stories of what it was like when known lesbians were dragged out of their dorm rooms to be committed to a mental institution before 1973 to discussions of competing in the upcoming Gay Games VII.

Amber and I met at that gathering. Both of us were in committed relationships at the time. Our acquaintanceship continued when we would run into each other at L-Word watch parties or other celebrations.

Then, in January of 2008, while registering students for class, I'd just finished telling my friend and coworker, Kelly, that I would only be open to dating one person. But, it wasn't possible because she was in a committed long-term relationship with her partner. Within half an hour of my mentioning her to Kelly, I answered a call from a number I didn't recognize on my cell phone. It was Amber. She said she'd gotten my number from the couple who owned the house where we'd first met. They gave her my number after she said she thought I'd be a fun person to hang out with.

I looked at Kelly and mouthed to her that it was Amber and that I would take the call. Her jaw dropped, and she shooed me away to talk in private.

During the conversation, Amber mentioned how sorry she was to hear that Kika and I had broken up a year ago. Then, she said she and her partner broke up six months ago and asked if I wanted to hang out. I said, "How about dinner and a movie?" She agreed.

We immediately learned that we shared a love for playing basketball and for animals. Ty-chi and her dog, Emily, got along as well as we did. Amber and I continued dating and made a pact that we would learn to do things the other loved. I learned how to snowboard, and she learned how to dance salsa. When I stayed at her place in Taos, I'd pack my dog Ty-chi, my cat Raisin, and Beta fish Mulan in my truck to go up that winding road from Espanola to Taos.

I enjoyed the conversations we had. She was passionate about teaching elementary school and was well-respected in her field. I implemented many of her teaching techniques and ideas for student engagement in my classroom settings. I wasn't a trained educator. I was a chiropractor who was passionate about health and healing. I enjoyed working as a chiropractor and loved teaching people options for better health. I wanted to continue my education to include animals in my chiropractic practice.

I saw the experience with Buddy as a gentle directional nudge from God and committed to the six-month Animal Chiropractic Program at Parker Chiropractic College. Becoming an American Veterinary Chiropractic Association (AVCA) Certified doctor was the way to go about it with the most integrity. Licensed chiropractors and veterinarians who satisfactorily finished the program took a board exam and, after passing it, became Certified AVCA doctors. It was a time and monetary commitment that was worthwhile.

My goal was to be of service while doing something I was passionate about.

Politics played a prominent role in the world of health care in general and health care for animals in particular. The law in New Mexico mandated that anyone who wasn't a veterinarian practicing chiropractic with animals must have direct supervision by a veterinarian to administer care. In 2006, I'd sent letters via regular mail to every listed veterinarian in the state of New Mexico with hopes of finding space to collaborate in well-rounded health care for animals. I received one reply from a veterinarian who thanked me for going about my practice legally, then said she did not need my expertise. Then, she went on to say she was retiring soon. I saw that as evidence that there was a need for holistic health care for animals in that state. After doing more research, I found that the need was worldwide.

I understood the insinuation in her letter about practicing legally because I'd had lunch with two chiropractors in the area who'd expressed their frustration that veterinarians were not open to chiropractors offering holistic care for animals. One doctor had tried to go about the process legally. Then, to the chagrin of veterinarians in the state, she did what she felt was the right thing and practiced anyway. Pet owners and caretakers didn't always know the politics. People merely expressed a need and desire for holistic animal care. Since they sought it out for themselves and experienced the benefits, they also sought the same healing for their beloved animals.

The next logical step was to get certified as a chiropractor specializing in animal adjusting by an internationally recognized organization. It was a significant commitment of time, energy, and finances. I committed to the coursework. Amber committed to taking care of Ty-chi, Raisin, and Mulan. In March of 2008, I began the program. By the end of 2008, I was a Certified American Veterinary Chiropractic Association Doctor.

I gained lifelong friends and felt a sense of belonging amidst my peers while taking that course. Becoming a Certified AVCA Doctor was satisfying, life-enhancing, challenging, and fun.

I felt grateful Buddy showed up as a metaphoric answer when I questioned which direction to move next. I felt fortunate to have had support from my roommate, to remain aware enough to read the signs, and to be inspired enough to take appropriate action. Confidence, focus, and energy were required to complete my plan.

Chapter 17

Winter 2009-2010
Taos, NM

Aries Rising says, "Only about twenty more minutes, and we're done."

Twenty minutes later...

Aries Rising says, "Almost done."

"I lost focus on that leaf half an hour ago. How does it look?"

Amber shares, "It looks nice!"

"Okay, all set. Let's take a short break. Then, you're next, Amber," Aries says.

"Okay."

Aries leaves the room while I put on my quarter-zip black long-sleeve shirt with a green pinstripe down each sleeve. Endorphins coursing through my veins, I glance up at the clock. Three and a half hours have passed.

Amber smiles and says, "It looks nice. I'm excited!"

"Me too! Doing a breathing visualization helped me remain grounded in my body. As I breathed in, I was mindful of coming home into my body. As I breathed out, I'd release the pain and relax. Maybe it will help you too."

"How do you do the breathing exercise? I'm still new to this woo-woo stuff, but it does seem to work for you, especially with the oils. I'll try it," Amber concedes.

I shared the process of visualization. "Picture yourself walking up to a small, peaceful body of water surrounded by a beautiful forest. Let yourself smell the scent of flowers in the air, see birds' colorful wings, and hear nature's sounds. Be there with all of your senses. Slowly walk into the warm, still water so you can stand, and the water comes just above your upper lip. Next, watch as a leaf falls from one of the trees onto the still water. The sounds persist and are relaxing - the leaf lands in front of your face. As you breathe in, the leaf gently floats toward your face. As you breathe out, the leaf gently floats away from your face. Breathe in. Breathe out. Focus."

2 1/2 hours later...

"That looks nice," Aries Rising says.

"Awesome!" I'm smiling ear to ear.

Then, Aries says, "I practiced on Denise. The second one went a lot faster. This one only took two and a half hours. Endorphins usually last three hours."

"Let's make sure these tattoos connect," I say. Amber stands in front of me, facing the same direction. I move closer until our bodies connect. I check to ensure that our tattoos align.

Aries offers, "They connect."

All three of us smile. Both Amber and I are emphatic. "Thank you so much!"

Each tattoo is individually unique and complete. Yet, when we stand together facing the same direction, the individual pieces connect and form a metaphoric circle, offering greater depth, literally and figuratively. Two perspectives function as one complementary unit.

Both tattoos display the phrase *Levity & Power Through Grace.*

My tattoo covers my back like artistically applied brush strokes. One end comes to a point over my right ovarian region. The other end terminates over my left shoulder, approximately three *cun* beneath my left clavicle midpoint. One *cun* is commonly used to find acupoints in Traditional Chinese Medicine and measures approximately three fingers in breadth.

Amber's tattoo covers the front of her torso. The top portion drapes over her left shoulder, terminating at her left shoulder blade. The other end is on her right *gluteus medius*, below her pelvic bone. The symbol at Amber's solar plexus is a straight line encompassed by a spiral moving upward and spanning its length. It almost looks like a slinky with a stick in the middle.

I have something similar to the familiar medical symbol of a caduceus around thoracic vertebrae 8, 9, 10, and 11. The unique symbol in my tattoo represents two complementary healing systems, having vision through one lens. Not only is this symbol at the core of my tattoo, but it's also at the core of my beliefs. Interestingly, this portion of my tattoo took the longest to heal.

The symbol and the region it's tattooed on are metaphors for the bridge that connects the science behind Western Medicine and Traditional healing systems. The best way to describe these interwoven concepts is by sharing a train of thought that highlights short excerpts of information and toggles back and forth between anatomy and physiology and holistic concepts.

The celiac nerve plexus is located in the solar plexus region of the body. This bundle of nerves contains a well-balanced combination of nerve fibers with opposing and balancing functions. They are found throughout the body, but we will focus on the solar plexus region during this train of thought exercise.

They are part of the fight, flight, or freeze internal mechanism. One set of nerve fibers, the sympathetic, automatically sends out a cascade of molecules when you sense you are in danger. This response affects every organ system of your body. The body primes to remove itself from danger quickly. Our blood pressure rises, and our heart rate increases. Blood shunts away from the digestive system and to the muscles. We feel more alert and focus on details in our immediate surroundings for safety. It's difficult to see the big picture and notice beautiful scenery when you are in a fight-or-flight state. That can become a mindset when your sympathetic nervous system is chronically active.

The opposing set of nerve fibers, parasympathetic, completes the cycle with a calming effect on our organs and state of being once the danger is removed. Our blood pressure lowers, and our heart rate slows. Blood is shunted out of the muscles and to the digestive system.

We feel calm and, often, grateful. We see the beauty in our surroundings and lives because we have time to look at the big picture - our mindset changes to one of hope. We can plan, respond, and choose a path.

The celiac plexus communicates with the kidneys and adrenal glands through these nerve bundles. Adrenal glands produce short- and long-term stress hormones, adrenaline and cortisol, respectively. The kidneys balance water and electrolytes, eliminate toxins, and produce hormones that regulate bones and white and red blood cell production. These paired organs are located in the same body region, the solar plexus, with one of each pair on each side of the spinal column.

In Traditional Chinese Medicine, the kidneys and adrenal glands are part of one of five elements, or phases of natural health, called the Water Element. Characteristics of this Element include being able to go with the flow, drumming up more courage than fear, generational qi, and prosperity.

Going back to the anatomy of the solar plexus region, there are five more organs I'd like to mention. One organ filters blood and aids our immune system, the spleen, and four digestive organs, the pancreas, stomach, liver, and gall bladder. All are located beneath the diaphragm, a sheet-like muscle necessary for breathing. I want to draw a connection between anatomy and Traditional Chinese Medicine. The spleen, pancreas, and stomach are on the left side of the body and are Earth Element organs in Chinese Medicine. The liver and gall bladder are on the right side of the body and are Wood Element organs.

Each set of organs is a reminder to live in the dynamic balance of mindfulness and inspired or planned action from both perspectives of anatomy and physiology and Traditional Chinese Medicine. When we are mindful of our food choices and take the time to prepare and sit down to eat a delicious meal, we set up our pancreas, stomach, and liver for success. Do you notice the difference in your energy level and your family's health when you prepare your favorite meal and sit down to share your day with your loved ones? That act of love sets up our pancreas, stomach, and liver for success so the nutrients we eat can be used as energy. The stomach digests protein needed for solid functioning muscles and the immune system. And the liver has over five hundred functions, two of which are releasing enzymes that digest fat and repairing and recycling cellular components required for a healthy body. Also, preparing and eating that delicious meal with loved ones delivers optimal nutrition to all your body's cells and stimulates the parasympathetic nervous system. And when do you get your greatest ideas? When you slow down. Gut instincts and the digestion of ideas lead to clarity, confidence, and good decision-making. It's all about balance.

Good nutrition leads to healthy organs and blood.

In Western Medicine, the spleen purifies red and white blood cells. In Traditional Chinese Medicine, a healthy spleen yields healthy muscles and a vigorous intellect. When we exercise regularly, we have a healthy immune system. Both schools of medicine teach the same thing using different terminology.

Going further, science confirms that we can increase the number of mitochondria within our bodies with endurance training. The highest concentration of mitochondria within the body is found in the muscles and the liver. Higher numbers of mitochondria increase adenosine triphosphate (ATP) levels. ATP is the currency of the cell that can be manufactured with or without oxygen. We manufacture two ATP from one glucose (sugar) molecule without oxygen. However, when we add oxygen to our ATP-manufacturing abilities, we can produce twenty-six to twenty-eight. Mitochondria are the workhorses for aerobic reactions through the citric acid cycle and electron transport chain. (Memme, 2021) I wonder if the electrical impulses generated through the electron transport chain and cellular metabolism throughout the body correlate to energy flow through acupuncture points and meridians. Is it possible that that is another link between science and traditional systems of healing?

When we contract a muscle fiber, we need one ATP and two ATP to allow a muscle to relax.

As we breathe in, we oxygenate tissues, improve our ability to make more energy, decrease pain, and feel grounded in the body. As we breathe out, we eliminate waste, regulate acid-base balance by exhaling carbon dioxide, and relax.

Breathing exercises are a part of many spiritual practices. The diaphragm is a sheetlike muscle that occupies most of the solar plexus region. When we inhale, the diaphragm contracts and moves downward, massaging our earth and wood element organs. The diaphragm relaxes as we exhale, and those organs can refill with healthy cellular fluid because we eat a nutritious diet and exercise.

Our bodies are wonderfully designed. When we combine the anatomical, physiological, and metaphorical constructs of form and function, the interpretation of health becomes much more interesting and enjoyable. By bridging both perspectives and viewing health and healing through one holographic lens, we can make sustainable daily lifestyle choices targeted for dynamic balance.

Chapter 18

To know when something or someone is out of balance, we must first know what a healthy internal and external environment is. Early signs of imbalance are almost always present for everyone and everything. Awareness is the key.

Awareness and presence are among the most helpful tools for practicing Post-traumatic Growth (PTG). It doesn't matter how you practice being mindful. What's important is that you practice paying attention daily.

Ancient systems of health and healing relied on observation of nature and internal mechanisms of the body. Many cultures around the world developed and adapted to how they interacted with their internal and external environments. Individuals and communities used plant and animal medicine. The systems of healing that evolved from natural law predate modern science and are time-tested.

Modern science brought information and options for longevity and survival. New details and understanding from scientific data were the catalyst of updated farming and cultivation techniques, greater success with surgery, and life-saving pharmaceuticals. Even with these benefits, science isn't perfect. It continues to evolve and make discoveries each year.

Some, if not most, of these discoveries stem from traditional cultural practices. For example, digitalis is a pharmaceutical that treats some heart conditions. Traditional forms of medicine, such as Ayurveda or Traditional Chinese Medicine, which are thousands of years old, passed information from generation to generation that the leaves of the common foxglove plant could be ingested to help alleviate heart conditions. In time, practitioners derived more effective formulas for each condition and evolved into current practices of holistic systems of medicine.

I prefer the holistic approach because when we use the whole leaf or part of the plant, traditional practitioners discovered it was most helpful, we gain the additional benefit of cofactors built into the constitution of the plant or part of the plant. Plants applied in this way, whether medicinally or nutritionally, are a well-balanced way to regain health. The effect isn't as dramatic as with more potent pharmaceuticals, and neither are the side effects. When scientists extract one active ingredient from the plant and magnify the amount administered, it could cause an imbalance in other organ systems. That may require trying to balance the side effects with additional drugs. Magnifying the original dosage of the active ingredient without the other balancing cofactors is like trying to spell "team" with an "I." The teamwork from the ingredients fortified by natural law, or God, is dispelled.

Many traditional medicine formulas embedded a spiritual approach into the practice and culture. Sustainability is built into many ancient holistic approaches to healing by only harvesting the plants so they may continue propagating. This helps ensure the survival of the plants used to help heal, and the community depends on the healing the plants provide. Many Indigenous teachings encourage the survival of seven generations. In other words, it was simple economics where the end was thought of while harvesting for current needs and sustainability.

The phrase *where attention goes, energy follows* is beneficial in helping one understand divine guidance. These phrases are two sides of the same coin. We can use these concepts when moving toward a destination or in a direction, and we can use these concepts when healing from a traumatic experience.

When Amber and I first started dating, holistic healing was a foreign concept for her. Like any exceptional educator, she observed when a change occurred. She watched me practice holistic methods of healing and witnessed positive health changes. She learned by listening and witnessing, which was the same way I learned to navigate my way with health and healing. I learned these methods from other holistic practitioners. And I watched her teaching methods and became a better instructor. We complemented and learned with one another.

In my case, I realized I'd made choices out of a reaction to traumas between the ages of four and eight, my formative years. As I got older and learned more about healing, I realized that I didn't have to go back over every detail of what occurred and how it affected my growth or my body's chemistry. I had to have the courage to feel and be in the present moment. In essence, it is a practice that Thich Nhat Hanh is widely known for, mindfulness.

The way I use this practice is to observe the way I feel throughout my body. I often do this when I first wake up in the morning. There is no judgment. I don't wonder why I feel that way. I notice how I feel and where I feel it. If I need to name something, I call it a sensation and leave it at that. It's a simple practice of listening to my body. It doesn't take long, maybe five minutes or less at first. Sometimes simply listening elicits a change in the tone of my health.

You can use the same concept when making choices throughout the day. You can reach for or think of something, and there will be a subtle shift in the sensations within your body and state of mind. Make choices that elicit a place of greatest balance. It is that easy.

Make responsive choices rather than reactive choices. A reactive choice would be out of habit, maybe a complaint because of something that happened long ago but isn't happening now. A responsive choice is a choice made out of what is happening at that moment.

This practice can be repeated throughout the day and applied to every situation. The path to a sustainable lifestyle is embedded within the ability to identify life patterns palpably. This conscientious and mindful practice may allow us to make whole-health-filled daily choices.

I learned a mantra from an Indigenous teacher that embodies this concept: "If isn't a *Yahoo Yes,* it's a *No!*

Chapter 19

October 4, 2015
Tiffin, Iowa

It was a surreal feeling sitting in that living room on our couch. The last time I'd felt settled was when Amber and I had first moved into our home on the south side of Santa Fe in July 2010. It seemed there hadn't been a moment to rest since I went in for that routine physical exam on October 13th, 2010. I still felt intense pain from head to toe daily since my doctor pressed over my right ovarian region. I no longer named what I felt pain. Instead, I called it a sensation. I had varied sensations throughout my body and varied residual effects from all of those transient ischemic attacks, the last of which was September 8th, 2015, a month before moving into this apartment.

If you looked into my eyes, you might have noticed I was neither alive nor dead. I could remember emotionally intense events but not the dates at first. I had to look at pictures, social media posts, emails, or bank statements to help piece them together. I felt uncoordinated and had difficulty putting sentences together. I could add and multiply, but I couldn't subtract or divide numbers in my head. Amber and I were beginning to reconnect. She was hyper-diligent and tuned in to our family's needs, how seasoned caregivers are. The PTSD was real and present for all of us.

We moved into the apartment about two weeks before October 4th. The metaphors around us reflected every aspect of our situation - the walls were void of artwork. There was wood veneer flooring devoid of rugs and carpeting. The sound echoed off the art-barren walls and floor, similar to how past events echoed in our actions. But there was also hope. The new construction apartment building we lived in was a work in progress. Five other units were still being completed within the same building. And I could look through the bedroom window outside at another building under construction.

We were fortunate to find this space. We'd looked at many apartments and had gone through five written pages of listings before finding this one in Tiffin, on the outskirts of Iowa City. I'd had difficulty breathing in almost every building we'd entered, including the one Amber worked in. I could breathe better outside. I spent much of my time outside or near a window. This second-story unit had a sliding glass door and balcony. They accepted pets. We still had one dog and one cat, Buster and Bruce.

The apartment was only a few miles away from Amber's three-quarter-time teaching position at a local elementary school. The day we were accepted as tenants, she'd driven us from uncle Bops and aunt Ahma's house in Cedar Rapids to Iowa City. I'd driven from the school to the apartment to wait for our new bed to be delivered. We'd stopped at the apartment, so Amber could carry in the cat tree. I carried the lighter boxes in after she'd gone to work.

It was easy to take inventory of our physical lives. We had our clothes, each other, Buster, Bruce, a cooler, a cat tree, and a sixty-six-liter plastic bin filled with items that triggered transient ischemic attacks (TIA's) for me. We'd whittled out a few items after Amber showed symptoms that mirrored mine. Interestingly, the acupuncture point sequence that Dr. Smith taught me alleviated my symptoms immediately alleviated Amber's dizziness, weakness, coordination loss, balance, and headache. Her health event followed a strenuous sprint workout and exposure to the same items, triggering a cascade of symptoms in me, Buster, and Bruce. Amber went to urgent care the day that happened. She had a follow-up appointment at the University of Iowa's Integrative Medicine Department, one of the three reasons we'd moved from New Mexico to that area of Iowa. We'd also moved there to be closer to family and access nutritious farm-grown food.

I'd decided to move from New Mexico to Iowa immediately after my Akashic Record reading with Linda Howe. I'd given Amber an out, saying she hadn't signed up for this whole sick wife thing, but I'd decided to go. It was my instinct that I needed to move, whether as a last resort for me to heal or for my family and friends to be able to say goodbye to me if I was on my way out. Amber decided to move with me. We did some research together and discovered a fourth reason to move - Iowa had excellent teaching opportunities for educators with Amber's experience and impressive credentials. Somehow, with much perseverance and by acting within our means and abilities, we found a safe place in Tiffin, Iowa, to land and digest all the experiences we'd had during the past several years.

One day, I sat on the cooler, looking out the open sliding glass door overlooking our detached garage and distant farmland, chewing on the fact that I trusted my instincts and was safe. The sounds of construction on the other five units echoed in the living room. I was sitting next to the cat tree, waiting for our mattress to arrive. It was a gift from my mom. She'd also gifted us a set of knives, dishes, eating utensils, stools so we could eat at the kitchen counter, and cookware. We had support in our renewal. We were very fortunate indeed and grateful for the love and support of family and friends.

Our future was unknown. How could we move forward and change our mindset from one of PTSD to one of Post-traumatic growth and success?

In that moment of mental chewing, I took inventory of what we had and reflected on the trail we took to get there. We'd applied the concepts from DreamWeaving to our health, relationship, and a cross-country move. Perhaps we could also apply it to rebuilding our lives. We had each other and the support and unconditional love from our family and community. We had our cat, dog, and our clothes. The plastic bin included our laptop computer, camcorder, and the two-hundred-plus hours of videos from the 2013 DreamWeaving Certification Course. And I had begun writing the bones of my book about a month before moving into our apartment, the day after the last TIA, September 8th, 2015. The most important things were that we had each other, support, and the wherewithal to move forward.

I supposed we'd take one step at a time and remain mindful, so we made choices that surpassed survival into fully living.

DreamWeaving Notebook

<u>Plus (+)</u>

- Open-minded and creative
- Sensitive
- Educated life-long learners
- Unique, connecting tattoos

<u>Delta (△)</u>

- Need for greater awareness and stillness - yin
- Running from feeling
- Too yang - imbalanced

<u>DreamWeaving Assessment - train of thought</u>

- Feel - Earth element - spleen/pancreas + stomach
- Stand in confidence and embrace the responsibility of living true to my holographic personality
- The pain kept me grounded
- Never settle - keep clear, authentic goals & a balanced strategy to attain them
- Healing and spirituality are badass and require grit and courage
- Actions speak louder than words - stillness feels louder than words

Solution: Release internalized trauma by staying calm, paying attention to thoughts and emotions, and instilling appropriate, balanced action and rest.

The message of hope: good communication breeds healthy relationships and unity.

SECTION 4

POWER

Authentic presence fuels exponential influence

Chapter 20

The word *power* takes on many meanings when defined in different arenas. Politics, math, science, social science, military, sport, and religion define this word from different perspectives. Power is a noun and a verb. The common link between each perspective of power is the freedom to choose our attitude and actions amidst any circumstance. When those choices are infused with our values and purpose, we flex muscles of hope that ignite passion in our daily lifestyle. We gain happiness and strength of purpose when we engage in the power of choice during all times of our lives.

In October 2010, I received a notice in the mail from the U.S. Copyright Office that my curriculum for DreamWeaving had been approved. Much work, research, and experience went into its development. But real knowing, from the heart, comes from experience. What I thought would be a quick two-week bounce-back for my health turned into a twelve-year journey applying the philosophy outlined in DreamWeaving holographic healing to every aspect of my life.

I began an unexpected journey of self-discovery and change.

For the eleventh day in a row, I felt extremely fatigued, with intense muscle spasms and head-to-toe pain on the right side of my body.

That morning on the twenty-fourth of October in 2010, I went into the bathroom to shower. Amber delivered a glass of fresh carrot and ginger juice for me to drink and found me sitting on the toilet in a heap of pain with the shower still running. I couldn't stand on my own. I had debilitating menstrual cramps. That wasn't unusual. Menstrual cramps had plagued me since menarche and were the initial reason for my quest to find holistic solutions for my health.

Amber turned off the shower and helped me into the master bedroom. My body's condition and the recent test results my functional medicine MD had ordered were concerning. Amber called a few friends for help. A new acquaintance who was an oncology nurse stopped by. She'd seen this scenario occur with ovarian cancer patients and sat with us for a while. Her presence and kindness brought us peace of mind. After she left, Melaney and Arthur dropped off some homemade Yogi tea made with love and intention.

Knowing that I was sensitive to pharmaceuticals but eager to get out of pain, I divided a tablet of the lowest dose of diazepam into fifths. I took one of those pieces and some herbal muscle relaxants. I felt a tingling sensation underneath my scalp twenty minutes after taking them. Then, I felt relaxed for the first time since the intense pain began to grip me on October 13th. Some of the pain remained, but I was able to rest. We thought we'd found a solution to the problem.

The next day, Amber and I sat at our kitchen table, where we distracted ourselves with a thousand-piece puzzle of Rome's Colosseum. The news of the ovarian mass was disturbing, especially because I felt weak, fatigued, and in pain. She and I discussed that there was a possibility that I might pass away sometime soon, mainly because I'd decided not to have surgery and predominantly pursue holistic healing. I shared my wishes with her. It was a difficult conversation to have for both of us.

Later that night, Amber and I had a heated argument, which was becoming a regular occurrence.

Menstrual cramps flared up on the morning of October 26th around 4 am. I took another fifth of a tablet of diazepam. Something very different happened with that second dose.

Around 5 am, I couldn't move my body from the neck down, and there was a disturbing stillness within my organs. Then, I felt a lifting sensation, as if my spirit was attempting to leave my body. I looked sideways from where my head rested on my pillow and asked Amber to get some oils. Amber retrieved some essential oils and applied them to the right side of my abdomen, where I felt sharp pains. I asked Amber to press as hard as she could on both acupuncture points located at the junction between my first and second toes, Liver 3 (LV 3). I looked down and noticed my skin fluttering the way a flag dances in the wind, and I felt an internal shift. It felt as if my spirit had nestled back into my body.

She didn't want to leave me alone. But, she had to go to work to create substitute teacher plans and set up things for her classroom's Halloween party. Around 5:45 am, Amber called our friend, Niki, to ask if she would sit with me while Amber went to work for a couple of hours.

Niki drove forty-five minutes to our house and arrived at 7:00 am. Amber was making us breakfast. Amber and the dogs greeted Niki at the door. Amber was grateful Niki could help and offered to make her breakfast, but she declined.

Amber shared more details about what had happened and left me in Niki's care while she ensured her classroom was taken care of for the day.

By then, I could move my limbs and body again but was still bedridden. Niki sat by the side of the bed and came up with the idea of rigging up a voice-activated pulley system with a harness so I could let the dogs out should something like that happen again. We laughed. Our ideas got sillier by the minute. We laughed some more.

Niki asked my permission to do intuitive energy-body work on me. I agreed. She worked on my right leg, hip, middle and lower abdominal region, and neck. She shared her insight with me as I listened. I began to feel more relaxed and in less pain about an hour and a half later.

When Amber returned home from work hours later, Niki asked her for help doing more energy-body work. Amber agreed. They worked well as a team. I was grateful for their help.

Afterward, Niki shared the take-home message that I need to *be* my truth. I let that sink in.

Then, Niki and I shared the pulley system idea with Amber. She wanted to be the only one with the remote in case she didn't like the direction of our conversation. Then she could press a button and send me out of the room. All of us laughed. It is the best medicine.

Niki's presence changed the tone of our home from fear to happiness.

After Niki returned to her home, Amber ran hot water and helped me to the tub.

While I was soaking, my best friend Virginia called. Amber brought the phone to me and placed it next to where my head was resting against the plastic pillow suction cupped to the back of the tub. Virginia didn't feel well either. Her doctors were having difficulty diagnosing and treating her. She'd called because she sensed something was wrong with me. Even though she and I lived over a thousand miles apart, we had a strong connection. Both of us made a pact to live our individual truths. After Virginia and I hung up, I felt optimistic, determined, and hopeful. I was fortunate to have a loving wife and loyal, dedicated, supportive friends. I gave the rubber ducky floating in my bath water a playful nudge to remind myself to stay afloat and reflect a sense of joy.

I knew early on that the foundation of DreamWeaving was Self-Care. A practitioner has to be healthy to offer the best perspective for the recipient(s). On October 12th,

2010, Amber and I had begun a 1,000-day training of doing at least ten minutes of qigong.

One day while teaching a class at Northern New Mexico College, we discussed every person having a gift that they excel at. We all encouraged one another to be authentic and live our individual and collective truths. In that class, one student asked me if I thought DreamWeaving Technique was a gift only I could do or if it was teachable. The concepts of health were accessible to anyone. The unique part was my approach, which combined linear and non-linear analysis. All essential oil and lifestyle choices were individualized and harmonized with the recipient's culture, synergistically tailoring ancient wisdom and modern science to their constitution. I'd told the student I didn't know, but I thought everyone could practice DreamWeaving.

The earliest form of DreamWeaving began in 2001 when I was holistically addressing my right breast mass. I weaved the imaging exams' science with time-tested meditation, exercise, and breathing practices. After Virginia introduced me to good-quality essential oils, I added the scientific and folkloric benefits of layering essential oils on my skin. I incorporated Dr. Sue Brown's teachings from Network Chiropractic seminars I'd taken while attending chiropractic school. I learned how the strength of the community brought about a depth of healing when working at Karen and Diane's house. That's where I witnessed firsthand the amount of conviction and commitment required to attempt to heal breast cancer holistically. I'd met authentic people, and they touched my heart deeply. They inspired me to integrate all the things I'd learned from and with them and transform them into DreamWeaving. Their teaching methods influenced how I taught DreamWeaving. It took all those experiences and two decades to distill what I'd learned into something I was passionate about teaching.

The first class I taught was at Virginia's holistic horse ranch. Amber went with me as tech support. She'd learned the concepts of DreamWeaving over the weekend.

Then, several months later, after I had an adverse reaction to the second dose of diazepam, Amber designed and delivered an aromatherapy application that helped me turn a corner in my mind, body, and spirit. She did it with a unique style to her specific skill sets and inherent gifts.

I realized, at that moment, that I loved practicing the hands-on aromatherapy application of DreamWeaving and that I could teach it.

Chapter 21

Animals have taught me that body language, energy, and behavior may be the best tools for understanding one another.

During a networking lunch in Santa Fe, I met Andrea Dewey, a vibrant and colorful woman. She owned the Canine Social Club, a boarding and daycare facility in Santa Fe. Andrea shared information about her business during our lunch, and I shared my healing journey and information about DreamWeaving. Fortunately, I'd found a legal way to work on animals in New Mexico.

I provided palliative care using DreamWeaving for one of her dogs during his last days. He responded well, and Andrea was grateful for my work. She asked if I could help with Jackie. I told her I didn't know and would do what I could.

The first day I met Jackie, September 8th of 2011, he was crumpled in a corner and shied away from looking people in the eyes. But this sixty-two-pound, ten-year-old neutered black Shar-Pei/Lab/Pit Bull mix knew exactly where I was and what I was doing.

Andrea shared Jackie's history and test results with me in the foyer of Canine Social Club in Santa Fe amidst vibrant wallpaper and animal-themed wall hangings. He'd been abandoned in someone's yard. When he was found, his chain was embedded underneath the skin of his neck. Jackie was rescued by a woman who had another dog boarding facility in Santa Fe. She brought him to Andrea's facility before vacationing and never picked him up.

Andrea took him to the veterinarian. Tests revealed Jackie had an enlarged spleen five times the normal size and presumed to be cancer. Jackie was slated for an expensive surgery, a splenectomy. The prognosis after that is usually an extended life of a few months.

I observed his behavior, posture, and gait. Then, I chose a bottle of essential oil that might help based on his history and my observations and partially opened it. Jackie licked and chewed, then glanced in my direction. I allowed a drop to fall on the palm of my hand and reached out to pet him with the back of my hand. He let me touch him. I relaxed. He relaxed, let me apply the oil, and I made a few gentle contacts, called disbanding, along his spine. He licked and chewed again, showing nonverbal cues that there was more ease in his system. Patience and kindness were the messages I'd hoped to convey with my intention and gentle touch. My work focused on helping to restore balance, then allow his body to do its healing.

I returned each week for nine weeks in a row to provide care for Jackie. Andrea shared what she'd noticed regarding his behavior each week. I observed changes in demeanor, posture, and gait. Then, I assessed his body using gentle touch to assess stress or ease within his nervous system, fascia, and muscle patterns. Were there changes in his head carriage or eye contact? What changes, if any, could I detect?

I paid particular attention to his reaction to specifically targeted essential oils. If he turned his head away when I opened a bottle, I took that as a 'no' and tried another oil or combination of oils. We all worked as a team and adjusted accordingly for Jackie's benefit. After each canine DreamWeaving session, I documented changes in behavior, oils used, areas where disbanding was done, and his responses.

Each week Jackie showed progressive signs of overall healing. He was more social with his canine peers and started walking over to me when I entered the foyer. And he looked directly at me. His entire system was more flexible, responsive, and accepting of less input. Plus, he appeared to have more confidence in how he held his head up.

How could I know if there was measurable change without scientific or empirical evidence? I asked Andrea to take him back to the same veterinarian to reassess him.

I was shocked when the ultrasound indicated that his spleen was clear and had completely returned to its normal size, and his kidneys were clear too! I didn't know there were issues with his kidneys. I'd read his veterinarian's SOAP notes and examined the imaging studies. Jackie received regular veterinary care and tests. I focused on doing what I could with him - helping balance his system so it could heal itself. I had knowledge, abilities, the owner's compliance and participation, and quality essential oils. I earned Jackie's trust. His body did all the work.

In the spirit of sharing is caring, I'm including Jackie's DreamWeaving Aromatherapy Application Chart. (See Appendix 3)

Jackie inspired us all. DreamWeaving helped Andrea save money and spend more years enjoying Jackie's companionship. She paid less than $500 for ten weeks of canine DreamWeaving Aromatherapy Applications. He lived another six years, happy and healthy. That's more than five and three-quarters years beyond his prognoses. Additional time with our loved ones is priceless.

Andrea talked. Because Andrea spoke with many people, my business grew via word of mouth into packs of regular customers who loved their animals. Barbara and Michael's pack would welcome me with wags at the door and escort me to the couch. Each dog would jump on my lap while the others patiently awaited their turn. The dog on my lap would face their back to me and jump down when they were done. Then, the next in line would jump onto my lap, and so on, until I'd worked with all of the dogs.

In Kristen's pack, Poco had an adorable way of choosing oils. I'd choose several bottles of oils based on Kristen's description of his behavior and ailments. Then, I'd place the bottles on the floor. Poco would sniff-test each bottle and enthusiastically roll on the bottles of oil he preferred. I'd swear he had a smile on his face during the oil roll. He was pawsitively adorable.

An equine regular was Biscuit. Biscuit's mom was a retired teacher who loved horses, New Mexico, and hiking as much as I did. I loved visiting her adobe house with scenic views of the mountains in Ojo Caliente. We'd talk and head out through the barn to the paddock to focus on Biscuit, whom she loved and took great care of. The paddock was fenced in and had a shade tree on the north end. Based on Biscuit's behaviors, palpation, and gait assessment, I'd offer her a selection of oil bottles. She "chose" her oils by inhaling each oil's scent, then licking, chewing, and moving closer to the bottle. She removed an oil bottle from the herd by moving her head away. Nonverbal cues communicate quite a bit. After a few sessions, Biscuit took the reigns by positioning herself in front of me while I stood in one spot, showing me which areas to look for and areas of stress. I palpated the area, then disbanded as needed. When the session was done, Biscuit knew the session was done and walked away.

I learned many things and looked forward to each day I practiced.

That year was a crucial time for the development of DreamWeaving. I witnessed the laws of nature it was based on in action. Animals responded well to this work. They didn't have to wonder about, research, or believe in it to heal. They did what came naturally to them, and healing naturally occurred. Who knew living my truth could be so satisfying and so much fun?

Chapter 22

On November 1st, 2010, Amber drove me to the Imaging Center in Santa Fe. The tech escorted me back to the testing area while Amber read in the waiting room.

The tech started with the Chest MRI. She asked me to put my arms over my head. I did so. She asked if that movement was painful. I replied yes. I added that my arms were already going numb. The tech hurried her pace. She put a device in my hand and said I should push the button if I needed assistance. I said okay even though I wondered how I could press the button if my hands were numb.

I thought to myself, *the MRI should be easy, right? I could withstand getting a tattoo that took three and a half hours. It seemed reasonable that getting three MRIs should be easy.*

The thoughtful and kind tech performed the chest, abdominal, and pelvic MRI scans.

An hour and a half later, I walked into the waiting area, where I found Amber. She looked up from a magazine. I told her my arms had gone numb for at least forty minutes, and there were hot spots throughout my abdomen. When her hand touched my abdomen, she looked from where her hand was on my abdomen into my eyes. She stated that all that swelling and heat wasn't there before the tests. I agreed. Neither was the burning pain. I shared that I'd had an MRI scan before, for a back injury in 1991 or 1992, but wasn't in pain afterward.

The woman at the desk released me. Amber and I went home.

Test results arrived at Dr. Ann's office. She was my MD who practiced functional medicine. Dr. Ann shared a copy with me. There were cysts in both ovaries and debris in my right ovary, where the ultrasound showed a solid mass with a blood supply. There were also fibroids in my uterus.

I wondered if the four rounds of ingesting essential oil capsules were a catalyst for my body to change the findings of my right ovary and why those changes would occur. Nonetheless, I was pleased with the change in results.

Due to previous reactions to over-the-counter topical progesterone that Dr. Green had recommended, I was concerned about adding hormone supplements to my healing regime. The adverse effects of that prescription and my choice to ignore my instincts had lasting effects.

On Thursday, November 11th, 2010, I wrote a letter to Dr. Ann thanking her for her help. I shared that I felt much better since taking the vitamin D3, bromelain, thyroid glandular, and probiotic supplements. I felt my muscles engaging again, and my head, neck, and shoulder muscles relaxed the same day. I asked if she would help explain why that worked so well in my next appointment.

I hadn't started taking the cortisol glandular supplement and compounded DHEA yet, but I was going to add that as soon as it was available to pick up at the pharmacy.

I shared that I believed I'd found a common thread to all of the tests and my experiences. It was a peek into DreamWeaving philosophy. I saw the main issue as transforming fat into useful molecules, i.e. energy and hormones.

Also, I saw a common thread with different types of connective tissue in the MRI scan results regarding the fibroid in my uterus, scar tissue in my lungs, and thickening of the outer portion of my gallbladder. I thought the fatty masses in my ovary and liver, and the small opacities in both kidneys might also be a connective tissue dysfunction.

I was rolling with my train of thought. She'd been a guest speaker in Northern New Mexico's Integrative Health Studies classes, and I thought she could help piece this puzzle together.

The transformation from one form of energy to another was associated with Fire Element in Traditional Chinese Medicine (TCM) and could be associated with passion for living. Fat is a type of connective tissue known as sinew in TCM. Sinews are associated with the Wood Element. TCM associates the liver and gallbladder with the Wood Element.

Drinking water and taking baths helped tremendously. In TCM, the Water Element organs and aspects nourish the Wood Element organs and aspects.

I didn't know where to go from there. I'd hoped she could help me fill in the blanks with my train of thought.

My letter continued showcasing that the MRI impressions were incomplete. I requested that she have the imaging center give a volume for the right ovarian mass and verify the volume for the left ovary. I'd made a volume comparison between the ultrasound and the MRI to see if there were any patterns.

According to my calculations, the measurements for the overall sizes of the uterus and right ovary increased in volume by eight and fourteen percent, respectively. That seemed reasonable due to an MRI scan having greater resolution when compared to the findings with diagnostic ultrasound. But, my left ovary showed a volume increase of slightly over ninety-two percent. That seemed excessive. Was there a problem with the left ovary too? I wrote that I was happy to see that the uterine fibroid decreased in volume by fourteen percent. But, I was confused as to why there was a lack of information regarding the mass on the right ovary, only listing one of three dimensions. That mass and right ovary were calculated to be five times the size of my left ovary. I asked if it was possible to get a complete report and reiterated that I greatly appreciated her help.

I found a different application for DreamWeaving. It was my way of living. I felt hopeful. I was surrounded by love and support. I could see and feel improvement with the steps I was taking. I knew I was on the right path for me.

DreamWeaving Notebook

Plus (+)

- Embraced opportunities
- My actions reflected my truth
- Unique approach
- Resilient and creative
- Intuitive and focused

Delta (∆)

- Quiet about being in persistent pain
- Confusing circumstances
- Unknown causes of illness
- Unusual response to pharmaceuticals

Rx

- I needed to communicate better
- Practice patience and persistence
- Good relationships are the key to surviving and thriving

Solution: Laughter is the best medicine.

The message of hope: Inspire others by living your truth.

SECTION 5

THROUGH

Trust the process

Chapter 23

Some detours teach us valuable lessons.

I'd written my second letter to Dr. Ann on Wednesday, November 17th, 2010, six days after the first. I started it with a plea to return to work at the college part-time, at her discretion, either on Tuesday, November 23rd, or Tuesday, November 30th, 2010.

After making that ridiculous plea, given my health circumstances, I shared my experience after taking the prescribed compounded DHEA and cortisol supplement.

I relived the experience while I wrote the letter.

It was Thursday, November 11th, at 9:45 pm. I looked at the bottle. It was 0.5 me 10 mg DHEA. My doctor described it as a "baby dose." I was acting against my instincts, but it seemed rational, on paper, to take the hormone prescription because the functional medicine test results reflected my symptoms. So, I topically applied 0.05 ml of the prescribed 0.5 me 10 mg DHEA to my right wrist.

The following morning all of my previous symptoms became exacerbated, and new disturbing symptoms began. I decided to trust my physician and override my concerns and instincts. So, on Friday, November 12th, at 6:30 am, I applied another one-tenth of the prescribed dose of the hormone DHEA topically and orally ingested one tablet of the cortisol supplement. I immediately felt nauseous when I placed the tablet of the cortisol supplement in my mouth before swallowing. I immediately felt that something was wrong.

In the letter, I shared the after-effects in detail. I had insomnia Thursday night after having slept well the previous three nights. Within twenty minutes of Friday morning's dose, I felt brain fog, dizziness, weakness, and fatigue. My hair started falling out. My eyes became puffy, my right eye was more swollen than my left. I had a headache and severe memory loss and couldn't remember what I was saying mid-sentence. My nasal mucus became thin. All of my teeth loosened. I felt pain return to my abdomen, liver region, and right breast at a seven out of a scale of ten. Both of my breasts hardened, and both nipples changed shape. Inflammation reached from the crease of my legs and pelvis, my inguinal region, to the bottom of my right breast. I also felt increased pressure and pain in the right side of my lower abdomen, which dramatically increased in size overnight without excessively eating, and in a way that excessively eating one week couldn't cause. I had spasms on both sides of my neck, hip, and upper and lower back muscles. Before taking the hormones, I'd only had spasms on the right side of my body. I experienced heart palpitations and shortness of breath. There was spontaneous bruising on my right calf at the junction of my soleus and gastrocnemius muscles. And my joints became stiff and achy. I had no idea that two baby doses of a baby dose could dramatically affect my health in a distinctly negative way, no matter how well-intentioned the prescription was.

In the letter, I informed her that I'd discontinued taking the compounded DHEA medication and the cortisol supplement and that it had taken me three days to remotely regain my balance to what it was before taking those two prescriptions.

I thought back to how I hesitated to take anything drastically affecting my hormone balance because I'd applied an over-the-counter progesterone cream at Dr. Green's recommendation. I thought back to classes I'd taken in chiropractic college, where we learned the difference between the minuscule doses of hormones the body releases compared to the amount given in hormone prescriptions.

The effects were dramatic and immediate. I felt a fullness in my lower abdomen after applying the topical prescription. My doctor playfully chided me and said I was being prescribed the lowest dose, a "baby dose," and that I wouldn't feel much of an effect for two weeks. I reiterated that I was sensitive to medications all my life and agreed to try a portion of the dose she'd recommended. I chose to try those medications against every cell in my body, mandating that I listen to my instincts. I took full responsibility for my choices.

Twelve years later, I'm still recovering from that moment.

Twelve years later, I'm still grateful that I also shared in that letter that Amber gave me a forty-two-minute

DreamWeaving Aromatherapy Application and that since then, I had been regaining strength and clarity at a rate I'd never experienced before. I was doing qigong, walking short distances, not quite half a block, and dancing around the house for short bursts. I also told her I'd kept a daily log and journal of almost everything I'd done since the pain began on October 13th, 2010. That practice helped me remain mindful and track patterns of what worked and didn't.

Amber and I'd sat down at our kitchen table and made goals, as individuals and as a couple, on October 12th. One was to practice at least ten minutes of breathing meditation and qigong for one-thousand days.

One other thing was working, a thyroid glandular supplement. But, after the experience with the DHEA and cortisol supplement, I'd lost trust in that MD. And, after the letters I wrote, I suspect she'd lost confidence that she could help me.

There were lasting lessons in the choices I'd made. Vitamin D3 was a keeper, but hormone replacements were not. To my surprise, DreamWeaving was working the best for me so far. I didn't know how long that would last. That was a keeper.

A few questions remained in my mind. What was my body protecting me from, and why did it respond to each therapeutic intervention the way it did? Why were blood tests telling one story and functional medicine tests telling another? The functional medicine tests aligned with my symptom picture, showing signs that my body and mind had been chronically stressed, causing adrenal fatigue. That affected my digestion, immune system, hormone balance, and how my tissues and organs used energy. Why did that align with my symptoms? I felt perplexed. I'd never heard of or read about anything like what I was experiencing happening in any of the classes I'd taken or taught. It was simultaneously confusing and enheartening.

In December 2010, I returned to work part-time at the college. My vertigo intensified as soon as I walked through the door to the Health Sciences building. I walked into my office and sat down. Then, I got up and walked back outside, where I could breathe more fully, and my symptoms lessened slightly. Two Nursing Program directors came to my aid and expressed that they believed the dizziness was due to the stress of returning to work after being on FMLA for a month and a half. I didn't rule out that possibility.

I loved working with my team of colleagues at Northern New Mexico College and was committed to the students, the college, and the program. I'd taught the first Intro to Integrative Healing class. I'd been on the original community and curriculum committees and was an integral part of the team who formed and continued the Integrative Health Studies Bachelor of Science Degree program. We were passionate about what we were doing. Every faculty member taught information from books and real-life experiences as practitioners and physicians.

I tried to walk the dizziness off. It took all the energy and wherewithal I had to make it to class. Seeing my students distracted me from the discomfort and made my heart smile. They'd been following the syllabus while I was away. Joel proudly updated me with what they'd done in class. Needless to say, it was an emotional homecoming. My student's care forever touched me for what they'd learned and put into practice with the material in the syllabus and their lives.

I met Dr. Arti Prasad and Dr. Mary E. Smith during an Integrative Health Studies program trip to the University of New Mexico's (UNM's) Center for Life, an Integrated Medicine Clinic in Albuquerque. They were the founders. They established an innovative safe space where Western Medicine and Eastern Holistic modalities could best help their patients. Students and faculty immersed in the Integrative Health Studies (IHS) Bachelor of Science Degree Program were possibly aligning as a feeder program to UNM Hospitals. Doors were opening for massage therapists at UNM Hospitals, which had an Integrative Medicine rotation for their medical school interns. Every person at that meeting wanted our work to positively affect the lives of our peers, families, and communities. It was a pioneering meeting when you consider that the IHS program was the only Bachelor of Science degree in Integrative Health Studies in the nation at the time.

Chapter 24

IHS classes were popular for community members as well as degree seekers. Class offerings included an intro to integrative healing, human anatomy and physiology, pathophysiology, nutrition, herbology, homeopathy, aromatherapy, ethics, energy healing, historical uses of integrative healing, a research class, and others. People of different backgrounds, ages, and experiences came together to promote practices that benefited the common good and a wellness lifestyle.

A few days after I played in a student/faculty basketball game, an event/fundraiser for the Integrative Health Studies student-run club, I went to my doctor for a routine physical exam. That innocuous physical on October 13th, 2010, alerted me to serious health conditions and changed my life.

I shared my history, current symptoms, and goals with my MD, Dr. Ann. She took my vitals and proceeded with the exam. When she gently pressed on my right lower abdominal region, I felt severe pain simultaneously radiating and connecting up and down my right side to my right temple and right foot. After the exam, a nurse drew my blood, and Dr. Ann ordered tests. The physical exam was on a Wednesday. The pain persisted on Thursday. Friday, I had to leave in the middle of an administrative meeting. My muscles were spasming so intensely that it felt like they might tear off pieces of bone from their origins and insertions. I'd gone in with severe fatigue, constipation, pain in my right side and top of my right foot, right sciatica, and low back pain. It was shocking to go from being active to barely able to lift my cell phone in a matter of days. The first healing step was to accept my situation and have the courage to change.

I was torn between nurturing the program at Northern New Mexico College I'd been a part of building and finding a way to regain good health. The Integrative Health Studies Bachelor of Science degree program was prosperous. It grossed over $2 million and netted over $1.5 million in four years, even though there was little to no advertising. There were plenty of challenges to address, and faculty and staff did it together. It was a magical time and intriguing that the entire program ignited from an idea. We'd built something tangible using focus, trial and error, and tenacity. I felt loyal to the program, the college, and the community. Others could keep that program rolling. There was a slew of amazing and talented doctor-educators on the IHS faculty. I needed to align with my truth. To do that, my health needed tending to. I submitted my letter of resignation in February 2011 and set out to set up a seamless transition so anyone could run the IHS program.

I didn't want to leave what I was familiar with and had grown to love. But, my health worsened any time

I went to the college. I'd noticed the same trend with colleagues. Four out of five full-time faculty on the first floor were seriously ill. Three of us had tumors, all women, and one other person required neck surgery.

My tattoo reminded me of three things, teaching the first DreamWeaving weekend class, my marriage, and my work at the college. Amber and I got our tattoos during the 2009-2010 academic year when I felt I did my best and most influential work at the college, close to when Amber and I married.

While planning our second trip to teach another weekend DreamWeaving course, Amber and I realized we could legally marry in Iowa. It was one of six states to offer legal same-sex marriage in 2009, and Spirits Whisper Acres was only an hour and a half drive from the border of Iowa. I didn't think I would ever get the opportunity to get legally married in my lifetime. I had dreamed of it since I was a little girl, tomboyish as I was. We requested a marriage license in Iowa. Then, we made an appointment to get married by a Justice of the Peace in Clinton, Iowa. I wanted a big wedding with my family and friends there. We couldn't afford it, yet we would be in the Midwest, and we were hopeful friends and family could attend even though it was short notice. Iowa was within driving distance from our parents in Illinois, Ohio, and Wisconsin.

Unfortunately, everyone was busy and had other plans they could not change with such a short amount of time to prepare. That hurt. Nonetheless, we moved forward. Virginia was thrilled at the news and said she'd change her plans to be our Maid of Honor. That was a blessing.

While we were staying at Spirits Whisper Acres, I instinctively called a friend from college whom I hadn't seen in sixteen years on the off chance she might be available to be one of two more needed witnesses for our wedding, with one day's notice. She and her partner said they would meet us in Iowa the next day. We were happy to have their support and love.

The people in Iowa were kind, open-minded, and as happy as we were to be a part of this pioneering relationship adventure.

Amber and I got married in Iowa on June 29, 2009. I felt different after reciting the vows Amber and I wrote. After signing the Marriage Certificate, I felt more committed and excited to be part of history as one of the earliest gay couples to marry in the United States legally.

Being LGBTQ seems to stimulate the necessity of thinking outside of the box, so to speak. Family is a bond formed with love or blood.

Amber and I had chemistry for the first six months of the relationship. As with any relationship, concessions were made on both sides. We encountered challenges, as with any relationship. Two of our pets passed away within seven months of our marriage. One was my twenty-one-year-old cat Raisin. The other was her ten-year-old dog, Emily. Looking back, I see that's also the time my health started to make a steady and rapid decline. I didn't recognize the signs and triggers at the time the way I do now.

My final endeavor while employed at the college was to hand out diplomas on the stage to that year's

IHS program graduates. I felt hopeful, humbled, and vulnerable as I stepped down from the director position into a new role.

First and foremost, I focused on my health. That meant doing what I loved and nurturing my body, mind, emotions, and spirit. I paused and noticed my life was compartmentalized. I'd had my own part-time business in New Mexico since 2004 as a chiropractor. As a contractor, I facilitated high and low ropes challenge courses at Ghost Ranch in Abiquiu. Amber and I provided team-building for staff and school-age campers at Golden Acorns Summer Camp. I taught classes and spoke at seminars about healing, aromatherapy, and self-care. And I had full-time employment teaching at Northern New Mexico College from 2007-2011. How could I incorporate all of those things into one business?

DreamWeaving.

The first DreamWeaving Technique Certification Course began on July 22nd, 2011. I taught it in the home Amber and I'd bought in Santa Fe. Western Medical concepts of human anatomy and physiology were aligned with Traditional Eastern Medicine. Dr. Ruth H. taught Chinese Medicine concepts. I sought to teach with a unique and unified perspective, bridging science concepts and time-tested healing systems with equal respect.

I was transformed, and DreamWeaving was transformed.

New techniques emerged. A gentle effective fascial release technique, *disbanding,* was born. Shannon added *Window to the Soul* to the technique repertoire. We discovered DreamWeaving's signature pupillary response during the certification course. We noticed that the recipient would perk up and shine brightly when the pupils dilated. It became the best way for the mind, body, and soul to concur with our oil choices.

We found that a simultaneous two-person aromatherapy application was easier on the practitioners and magnified the recipient's global health benefits. We developed synergism.

As our skills and DreamWeaving became more refined, we used fewer drops of oil and got better results. The practice of DreamWeaving became cost-effective and sustainable.

We noticed that the body coaches and communicates its needs to us. We learned to interpret and translate body language. Then, measure pre- and post-aromatherapy application parameters to assess feedback and progress. Our science became an art, and vice versa.

I emphasized Self-care for the practitioner and recipient's safety and benefit. Self-care was also important for practitioners who didn't have access to effective treatment. They'd still have the option of using a wide array of self-healing practices, and they knew how to apply them effectively to several situations. The self-healing practices gave birth to the fitness application of DreamWeaving. I began to realize the depth and breadth of integrating and unveiling synergistic similarities of different perspectives of health and healing. And I loved everything about it.

I kept moving forward.

Chapter 25

Focusing on my interests allowed a domino effect of insight and growth.

In November 2011, Amber and I went to the American Veterinary Chiropractic Association (AVCA) Annual Conference in San Antonio, Texas. I attended the conference to meet continuing education requirements to remain a Certified AVCA doctor. Amber went with me for two reasons: she shared a love for animals, and I still needed help doing daily tasks. I had vertigo 24/7, fatigue, pain, and nausea - continued aftereffects after applying two doses of DHEA hormone cream to my wrist a year before the convention.

I met two people who would impact my life and the course of my healing for the rest of my life. I met Dr. Luke Cua and his wife, Irene, at their vendor booth. I'd signed up for treatment with this seventh-generation Doctor of Chinese Medicine. During my appointment, I shared my recent history. He checked my pulse, tongue, and pupils to make a diagnosis. After I told him about my experience with prescription drugs and that it felt like my organs had shut down, he rechecked my pulse. He skillfully pressed my radial arteries in various directions and with varying depths of pressure. Then he removed his fingertips, looked at me, and said, "You must still have things to do in this life."

Dr. Cua had his way of believing, confirming, or disproving what I shared with him. I'd heard of people who could read your history via pulse diagnosis, yet I'd never met anyone who could do it. I believed it was possible. I learned how to translate body language and the soft tissues surrounding the spine from Dr. Sue Brown when I took her courses while simultaneously attending chiropractic college. I used those assessment tools daily for my work with people and animals. Dr. Cua did his version of translating the truth based on his seven generations of knowledge. Dr. Cua also had a computer program in which he'd designed algorithms based on specific acupuncture points and electrical conduction quality. I got a visual printout of data collected from his computer program that aligned with traditional diagnostic techniques in columns and graphs.

He used tongue acupuncture to release stagnant chi and used his one-needle qigong technique. I bought the supplement formulas he recommended. I'd been trying supplements, and none had lasting effects besides Vitamin D3. I was open to new things. Dr. Cua's synergistic supplement formulations and treatment methods proved priceless.

Meeting Dr. Cua was a Godsend.

I identified and implemented key lifestyle choices for whole health healing. Symptom triggers revealed themselves as I tested my new finds.

Dr. Cua's supplements were pricy. Amber and I were implementing what we'd learned in a financial fitness class to decrease debt. One day I ran out of supplements and didn't place another order to save a little money. Three days later, the pain increased in my upper back, right side, and abdomen. My headaches worsened, and I could not stand upright due to severe low back pain. Amber and I drove to Colorado to spend Thanksgiving 2012 with Amber's youngest sister. I'd forgotten to bring external castor oil pack materials, so we stopped to pick up some supplies. I applied an external castor oil pack in the car and, later, at her sister's apartment. It helped decrease the pain temporarily. After that Thanksgiving visit, Amber and I drove back to Santa Fe.

After arriving home, the pain worsened. It was the worst headache I'd had to date. Then, my speech started to slur. I lost my balance and fell to the right. My right side became very weak. Amber called two doctors. They recommended that I go to the ER. I didn't go to the ER. Amber gave me a DreamWeaving Technique treatment. Eight hours later, the major symptoms subsided. The next day, I ordered my own CT scan without contrast. The report was short and stated that everything was within normal limits. I sent the CT scan in for a second opinion. He gave a more thorough report and mentioned opacities in the right vertebral artery and pineal gland. It was considered within normal limits for a woman of my age. I was forty-four years old. Honestly. How can that be?

A week later, I flew to Los Angeles to see family, take a class with Dr. Cua, and get acupuncture treatments.

My symptoms became exacerbated during the ascent and descent of the flight. And I don't remember getting on the bus or much of the *FlyAway* bus ride. But I arrived at Union Station, where my aunt picked me up for a visit.

When I arrived at my appointment, I told Dr. Cua what had transpired after Thanksgiving. He assessed my pulse and paused. Then, he brought me to a treatment room. I felt pressure at the base of my skull and heard a clicking sound, similar to a chiropractor's activator gun. Then, I felt a "pulling" sensation in the same spot. With each skillful treatment application, it felt like he pulled the pain out of my head. Then, he placed more acupuncture needles in my abdomen. He had six hundred years of archived knowledge as a seventh-generation Doctor of Chinese Medicine. He helped me in ways I didn't believe were possible. While I rested, I looked over at the counter and saw the suction device attached to a cup lined with my blood. I realized his version of an activator gun had needles attached to it. Several minutes passed as I relaxed. Dr. Cua checked in with me and asked if I was okay. I said yes. I felt much better. I found out later that what he did was a post-stroke treatment.

After that experience, I became a believer in the power of acupuncture in the hands of a knowledgeable and experienced physician, and I purchased supplements with greater confidence in the skill and care that went into their formulations.

I flew home to Santa Fe without incident.

I was pleasantly surprised that my symptoms became manageable. I'd gone from taking three capsules twice daily to five capsules twice a day. I was functional and could work.

I recognized I'd fared best with nutritional supplements formulated with synergistic whole-food ingredients. This was a new realization. I didn't take any supplements regularly before October 13, 2010.

You couldn't help but smile and laugh any time Buster was around. Buster was my connection with Virginia's character and generosity. Virginia rescued him from a kill shelter when he had thirty minutes to live. She was particular about who would become his forever home and concerned that he might be mistreated or that his very muscular Pitt body and loyal heart might be used to fight. At Spirits Whisper Acres, Buster spent most of his time learning respect and manners while outside, fenced in, with an alpha female Mastiff named Lady. During one of our visits to Spirits Whisper Acres, Amber and I took the two dogs out for a walk on leashes down to the river at Virginia's request. I paired myself with Lady. Amber took Buster Bu. As the four of us jogged toward the river through the high grass, Buster randomly leaped up high enough to look Amber directly in the eyes. Meanwhile, Lady was a perfect lady. When we all returned to the house, Virginia smiled knowingly at us. She knew we wanted to give Buster a home.

A few months later, Amber, Ty-chi, and I met Virginia outside Kansas City. It was the Summer of 2010. Ty-chi wagged her entire body when she saw Virginia. Buster immediately recognized us, made Buster Bu sounds, and wagged his entire body. Ty-chi sat next to Virginia and me and watched with a poised stare while Amber took Buster for a jog. His tan and white body resembled that of a Pinto while he did his best Lipizzan impersonation. All of us laughed and smiled. Ty and Buster met each other with sniffs, wagging tails, and happy faces. When we got to the hotel room, those two practiced canine team-building by tearing apart a pillow Virginia had brought from Spirits Whisper Acres. Buster Bu Man was accepted into our family.

During the drive back to Santa Fe, Ty and Bu snuggled in the back seat with one another. Amber texted a pic of them sleeping with their tails draped over each other's butts to Virginia.

Amber and I also adopted two kittens. Bart and Bruce, short for Black Bart and Bruce Lee. They were the cutest fluffy-faced brothers you could imagine. Bruce had a bit of attitude to his little black-and-white body. Bart was all black, love and cuddles, a real purr machine.

The kittens seemed to enjoy taunting the dogs, so we separated Bart and Bruce from Ty-chi and Buster. That lasted approximately two months. After Ty-chi passed away, Amber and I integrated Buster with the kittens.

Then, Buster started limping. Amber and I noticed a growth on his front leg that emanated heat. The mass proliferated and was in a common location for canine osteosarcoma. We took him to the emergency vet. $1,000 in tests later, we had no definitive answers. X-rays revealed a growth close to his paw on his front leg, what we would consider our wrist, that had an unusual composition - something the vet had never seen before.

She did a biopsy. It revealed white blood cells but no obvious malignant cells. She prescribed antibiotics and muscle relaxers.

Buster started panting, and his chest turned bright red after we'd given him the second dose of the antibiotics. The muscle relaxers had a strong effect on him too. He looked like a blanket conforming to the seat cushions of the couch. We stopped giving him the meds and checked in with our regular vet. She agreed it was best to stop them.

Next, we called a canine acupuncturist to help him. He relaxed during the treatment. However, the mass continued to grow aggressively.

We tried another option.

Amber had become a Certified Canine Massage Therapist at that time. She and I teamed up and provide DreamWeaving Aromatherapy Applications for our Buster Bu Man. We used resource books to choose oils that matched Buster's vibrant personality, health presentation, and history. (Higley 2010, Mojay 1997, Worwood 1999) Bu Man licked and chewed to confirm the oils. Then, we safely applied the oils to his fur. Next, Amber did the canine massage and fascial pattern disbanding portion of the treatment while I did the spinal balance portion. Amber and I were a great team.

I enjoyed witnessing Buster's entire body relax while his facial expression transformed from an adamant mug of a dog who'd chewed through almost an entire loveseat into one of an angelic, muscular, bully-breed cherub. The cats comforted and cuddled with Buster while he healed. The growth slowly dissipated, as did his lameness. Bart and Bruce tormented him again when Buster felt better. They got their exercise.

We had a happy household.

Enter Maharani. *Maharani* means "woman with beautiful eyes" in Sanskrit and is usually reserved for royalty. The only way I could look at this dog without crying was to look her in the eyes. Our client had asked us to check on her. Maha had been found wandering through an arroyo in Santa Fe. She was gaunt and dragging a broken chain attached to her collar. Her teats were swollen, and her uterus was prolapsed. She had skin hanging as if it had been stretched over her protruding skeleton. This red Pit mix was so weak she couldn't walk straight. Our client and her friend told Amber and me they'd called a veterinarian. Given her condition, the veterinarian didn't think she'd survive being vaccinated or live longer than two weeks. The two women posted signs in their neighborhood regarding this lost dog. When nobody claimed her, Amber and I brought her home. We aimed to help keep her as comfortable as possible and shower her with all the love she could receive for the remainder of her life.

We teamed up again and put towels on the massage tables used to teach the DreamWeaving Certification Course. Buster jumped up on the waist-high table. Amber lifted Maha onto another table. The two dogs received weekly canine DreamWeaving sessions. I enjoyed witnessing them relax, wearing peaceful expressions on their faces.

The owner of Marty's Meals in Santa Fe heard about our endeavors and donated human-grade, gently cooked meat for the dogs. We supplemented the meat with steamed organic carrots, kale, and rice or potatoes. The cats ate high-quality kibble and wet food. We added Dr. Cua's nutritional supplements as needed.

Buster's mass completely disappeared. Maha gained weight and strength.

My coworker from the college, Kelly, and I deepened our friendship. She and I shared similar symptoms. Both of us were extremely fatigued and in tremendous pain. We had difficulty eating and got full quickly. Both of us had painful bowel movements. Kelly and I exchanged ideas and tested holistic and integrative healing options. She and I discussed the toll illness took on our relationships. We commented on how difficult it was for each of us to function daily and that the people around us didn't know how much strength and wherewithal it took to get out of bed. Both of us had a raw sense of humor. We laughed at experiences we'd had that others without those experiences might consider inappropriate or horrific. We cried too. Much had happened between the time we fell ill in the fall of 2010 and May of 2013.

In early May of 2013, Kelly succumbed to cancer. Her doctors initially thought she'd had a benign mass surrounding one of her kidneys. The mass and one kidney had been surgically removed in December 2010. A few months later, clear cell carcinoma had seeded as cancer into her lung, which had deflated during the biopsy. She continued to go the Western Medical route. Then cancer spread to her brain, skin, tongue, and eventually into her bones. Like Virginia, Kelly kept telling me I should write a book. Like Kelly, Virginia succumbed to cancer in December 2010, when her doctors had difficulty identifying and treating it. I utilized the wisdom and knowledge they imparted to me. I'm grateful for the honest, grounded, heartfelt moments I shared with them. Both of them died as they lived - with courage, strength, and integrity. Their presence was priceless to me. I felt a void in my heart at the loss of these irreplaceable friends, especially in close temporal proximity to the loss of Abuelita. The people I'd confided in the most were gone. I missed their courage and direct opinions.

Amber's grandmother also passed away from cancer within the same three years. How does someone, or a couple, repair their hearts after such losses?

Amber and I had to find a way to intertwine a season of pain and grief with love and innovation. We'd begun a cycle of post-traumatic growth that spanned several years. We could never replace the loved ones we'd lost. We had to find a way to let go, move on and play. We'd decided to fill the emptiness with activities she and I enjoyed doing together. Since she and I loved playing basketball, we decided to recruit women of like minds to join a summer league basketball team. The incredible women on that team became dear friends.

Our summer league basketball team was much wiser than the other teams in our league. That is to say that the other teams were at least half our age. We were no spring chickens. Imagine a team filled with a conglomeration of cultures and careers who supported one another on and off the court. That was us. Practices were a great time to bond with Kate. Louisa was quietly supportive. Camille kept Amber and me looking fine with free hairstyles. Brenda let us use one of her songs as the background music for a Kickstarter video free of charge and donated jerseys to our team. Kateri was our loyal fan. We were tough as nails on the court and had a perfect record. We never won a game. Nonetheless, we always left the court smiling. We played for the sheer joy of playing. Don't get me wrong. We wanted and tried to win, but the other team always scored higher.

One of our team members, Kathleen, The Sound Lady, did voice assessments and sound healing for Amber and me. At first, I didn't know much about voice assessments and was unsure what to think about them. Kathleen explained that the readouts were based on math and frequency. Vibrations within the voice were calibrated to the frequency of the molecular weights of specific compounds. I was open-minded enough to try it. I was a kinesthetic learner. I'd received adjustments from Dr. Sue Brown regarding Network Chiropractic, which was life-changing. Interestingly, some of the information from the voice prints gave direction and showed early detection for medical tests done later. Heavy metals and a toxic exposure pattern appeared in both Amber's and my voice prints.

I researched and noticed further signs of heavy metals in my health presentation. I read as much as possible on the subject and discovered that there were blood and urine tests for such things. How would I know for certain unless I had medical tests done? That way, heavy metals could be confirmed or ruled out as contributing factors for my unusual symptoms, which continued to worsen. My theory was that my body would try to recover homeostasis and heal if I could identify and eliminate the cause.

In October 2013, I changed my Primary Care Provider. She ran blood tests, checked for occult blood in my stool, ordered an abdominal ultrasound, and requested a mammogram. Tests revealed similar findings to my voice print. Heavy metals were in my blood - arsenic, mercury, and lead. There was blood in my stool. And I was classified as BIRADS 4 after the mammogram and diagnostic ultrasound. BIRADS stands for Breast Imaging Reporting and Data System. The number 4 indicates a suspicious mass detected in the mammogram and diagnostic ultrasound. And I experienced a partial seizure immediately following the abdominal ultrasound test. I'd never had a seizure before. I'd been having unusual reactions to medical tests that would usually be a benign experience for most people and me. But, for reasons unknown, my body responded unusually. I looked healthy on the outside to the naked or uninformed eye. However, tests revealed unusual findings. I repeatedly heard the words "I've never seen anything like this before" at every doctor's visit. Every. Single. One.

My PCP recommended a colonoscopy. I refused that test because I'd had long-lasting, life-threatening reactions to the drugs I'd tried and wasn't willing to undergo worsening symptoms similar to what had happened when I took the diazepam and applied the DHEA cream. Another option was to have a colonoscopy without drugs. No, thank you. The thought of having a colonoscopy done without drugs was unappealing at best. One of the women on our basketball team had experience with that. After hearing her description of what transpired, I said no. There was the treatment aspect to consider as well. How would a colonoscopy result change my course of treatment if I couldn't take drugs? How could I have surgery or do chemo if a malignancy was detected?

Then, more questions surfaced. Why don't we have less invasive tests? Why are drugs required so often to make a diagnosis? Don't drugs alter physiology? How do we diagnose people and animals who are allergic to drugs? I was in a spot I didn't want to be in. But I had to look at and accept the reality of my situation. And my health condition affected other loved ones financially, emotionally, mentally, and physically. I had to accept either the path I was traveling down or pivot.

I wanted to make a difference in the world of healing.

The same month, I gave a talk at one of the pueblos for breast cancer awareness month.

The disparity of power and legal practice between veterinarians and chiropractors was out of balance. If people could seek holistic care, particularly chiropractic care, for themselves, why couldn't they legally seek holistic care for their animals without jumping through hoops and paying more? If I could put together a presentation that embodied a bridge between science and holistic systems, perhaps both professions could find a way to work together for the benefit of our animal patients. Earlier that year, I'd submitted to speak at the 2013 American Veterinary Chiropractic Association (AVCA) Annual Conference. I was thrilled to be accepted for a two-hour slot. My presentation was entitled *No Health No Practice*. It was an offshoot of the phrase *no hoof no horse*, which meant if the horse didn't have a healthy hoof to stand on, that horse would often have to be put down. I was a living example that if we didn't have our health, we wouldn't have the strength to practice.

In November, I presented for the first time at the AVCA's 2013 Annual Conference. I included team-building in my presentation and offered some self-care practices. My time as Director of the Integrative Health Studies Program at the college may have opened a door for me to present in a prime spot. Approximately two-hundred doctors from five countries would be in the same room together rather than in smaller break-out sessions. There was stadium seating. I felt exhausted and in a tremendous amount of pain. I went to Dr. Cua for two acupuncture treatments at his vendor booth before I presented and began to feel much better. I attended as many lectures as I could.

Before my presentation, I assumed a confident, open, and strong posture. (Cuddy, 2012) Familiar faces in the audience offered smiles of support. Some doctors in the audience had raised eyebrows as if to say, *what do you have to offer that I don't already know?* We started with booty script, or as one of the doctors called it, *ass*

DENISE M. MICHEL

writing. We wrote letters in the air with our butts to loosen up our joints and help people drop that dime they were squeezing between their butt cheeks. In the words of Loretta LaRoche in *The Joy of Stress*, we dropped some change. Smiles and laughter ensued. I shared my personal story, offered science and statistics, and talked about essential oils and qigong. Then, I challenged them to do the form of qigong I did daily. My challenge was accepted. Can you picture what it looked like to have two-hundred doctors lying on their backs with their feet and hands raised in the air on the writing tables of a lecture hall? They held the sleeping tiger yoga pose for five minutes while I guided them through the breathing meditation accompanying that core-strengthening exercise during that surreal scene. It's more challenging than it looks. I'd gained their attention. I offered more science and statistics. I emphasized that it was important that healthcare professionals were healthy. We discussed a few more self-care issues, and I started another team-building activity that demonstrated how it's possible that some essential oils could be effective against bacteria relative to antibiotics. We ran out of time to finish. A good number of doctors elected to remain for another twenty minutes. Most people left *No Health No Practice* with a smile and attended the banquet with camaraderie. I was still in pain, but I didn't mind. I was doing what I loved. I had a purpose. I shared some core principles of DreamWeaving.

When I returned home from the conference, I experienced an immediate decline in my health. I had difficulty breathing inside our home. I immediately started coughing when I opened the door to enter our home. A mass was visibly pushing outward from underneath my skin on the side of my right breast. It was growing noticeably larger, harder, and more painful by the day. My hair fell out from the roots, and I felt extraordinarily fatigued. I'd tried to figure out what the cause might be.

The previous year, on September 5th of 2012, the roof of our house had failed, and as a result, the walls buckled in the garage. The house's builders replaced the roof at no charge. However, they painted over water-damaged materials without replacing them.

A client lent us money to test our house for mold.

I'd read about faulty drywall. Our house had been built in 2004 during a red flag time for increased use of that product. There were possible similarities with the corrosion and blackening of the electrical wires in the house. The rubber tube that went to the ice maker of our refrigerator failed. One of the rubber tubes broke on our dishwasher, and the water heater had to be replaced before we moved in. Everything that went wrong revolved around water and the disintegration of rubber. High humidity was an issue commonly mentioned regarding problems with faulty drywall. Amber and I opted out of including those tests.

We decided to continue funneling our money toward holistic healing modalities, supplements, and essential oils. Those expenses were out of pocket.

The professional mold tests revealed quite a bit of mold in our house. Could mold cause my symptoms?

We investigated our options. Mold remediation was not covered in our homeowner's insurance policy. We met with an attorney. He said that Amber and I might have had recourse if a toxicologist had found the same substances in my body that were detected in our house. Is it possible that the body transforms mold into metabolites the way our digestive system breaks down food into molecules our bodies use as cellular building blocks and energy? That would have required an initial investment of $20,000 with our attorney and a substantial financial commitment for toxicology testing.

I contemplated our experiences and circumstances.

Dr. Cua's supplement recommendations worked while I was in Dallas. I didn't understand why I felt fine while traveling and worse at home. I would think the opposite would be the case.

One day as I rested, some realizations settled in. I'd had serious digestive issues and was beginning to bruise spontaneously in many areas of my body. Also, the cats started vomiting frothy hairballs. They also had diarrhea and unusual reactions to their medications after being neutered. After Maha was spayed and had some masses surgically removed, she took an antibiotic, and a mass emerged through her chest wall. Buster was throwing up a froth after he drank water. And Amber had a persistent infection.

All of us were sick. None of us responded well to pharmaceuticals. Were all of us having difficulty metabolizing drugs? If so, why?

I added more supplements to my plate, one at a time, until I found balance and functionality. I ramped up to taking twenty-three different supplements twice a day.

Then, I moved into a client's guest house on the north side of Santa Fe.

We received the official mold test results in a few days after I'd moved into the guest house.

Many things happened during my stay in that guest house in December 2013. I had three objectives: 1) increase my energy level, 2) try to get my body to halt the growth of the breast mass, and 3) enjoy life.

After I moved into the guest house, my health improved. I could get a whole night's rest. My energy level increased. The pain lessened. From what I could feel with palpation, the mass stopped noticeably growing. And my muscles began to engage again.

I read, walked, chopped wood, socialized with my client, and worked a little.

Amber had our car. She visited when she could. She stayed in our home and took care of our pets.

Chapter 26

A healthy nervous system is relaxed. When we experience stress, our adrenal glands secrete stress hormones, and our flexor muscles become tense and overactive. Your posture changes, so you are ready to move. Posture affects your neurology and its expression. Neurology affects physiology, which is the environment your cells bathe in and communicate with one another. All of it impacts your state of mind and vice versa. When the stressor is gone, the body's healthy response is to move out of being in a stress response back to being calm. It's a full-circle response that ends in resolve, reset, and renewal.

Dr. Sue Brown guided and helped me understand how to identify physical and emotional patterns within the body's tissues. The body's holding patterns resulted from a stressor that, in essence, had not completely healed and was stuck in the stress response. These patterns have different physical presentations. For instance, muscle and fascial tissue may have a boggy or rubbery feel or possibly a strap-like consistency to the touch. It took time and experience to develop the art of translating the body's language and identifying when and how to release these muscle patterns. The wider the pattern, the longer the individual had been committed to repeating a habit or *set in their ways*. It's a way of reading a cellular mindset.

I was driven to resolve neglected traumas to alleviate chronic pain. That's how I met Dr. Sue Brown. I'd read Deepak Chopra's books about quantum physics and quantum healing to understand what I was experiencing. I read Candace Pert's *Molecules of Emotion* to understand some of the physiological and psychological shifts I was experiencing. Louise Hay's *You Can Heal Your Life* added a metaphoric dimension.

When I started receiving adjustments from Dr. Sue Brown, I thought there had to be a strong physical force to affect healing. She used structural techniques that chiropractic is most commonly known for. But she also used low- or non-force techniques. Those techniques unearthed emotions and memories I'd buried and stored within my tissues. My muscle memory took more than an athletic tone. I realized my cellular memory included some emotionally and mentally traumatic events I hadn't resolved, evidenced by a resurfacing of emotions after chronically tense muscles were released.

According to Deepak Chopra and the writings of other holistic healing experts, the second law of thermodynamics also applied to our cells in that energy could not be created nor destroyed. It could, however, be transformed. And our bodies are masters at applying this transformation in the same way that nature adapts and harmonizes.

Assisting in the release of these patterns is an art. It cannot be forced without causing more harm than good.

A practitioner must recognize the perfect place, time, readiness, and release sequence to benefit the recipient or patient. Once appropriate patterns release, the body returns to a palpable state of ease. Dr. Sue taught me that as healing continued, underlying patterns become evident, and the process of identifying, uncovering, and removing layers of stress patterns continued until we returned to a pure and wiser expression of self.

Acknowledging and accepting warning signs was not always my forte. I'd spent much time in a chronic state of stress. Before the experience with transient ischemic attack (TIA) symptoms in November of 2012, I knew warning signs were there but didn't believe they would worsen. One doesn't have to believe in something for it to be true. I didn't believe Dr. Sue Brown's adjustments would help me, but they did. I also didn't think essential oils were therapeutic for me, but they were. And I didn't think Dr. Cua's supplements would make much of a difference, but they did.

Six weeks before my first TIA, I had a horrific headache and blew blood clots out of my right nostril every day for six weeks. The headaches were worse at my right temple. I felt as if I had been punched in the face repeatedly.

During that period of time, Amber and I were attempting to raise funds to publish a book entitled *The Soul's Whip*. We'd set up a Kickstarter campaign. Supporters shot and participated in a video promoting our project. (178natfue, 2012) One of the women on our summer league basketball team, G Precious, donated rights to one of her songs so we could use it in the video. Nathaniel, a former student from the college, shot, edited, and posted the video. Amber and I had much support and love coming in from many directions. In the video, I sounded stuffed up, and the right side of my face drooped. The signs were there for me and my doctors to see. I didn't know how to accept such subtle and not-so-subtle clues about what was to come.

The Soul's Whip was an unpublished tell-all book where Amber and I transcribed each other's journals and shared the results of my medical tests. If you're ever bored and want an entertaining evening, record yourself while you sit down with your spouse after you've been through serious circumstances and transcribe your spouse's journal while she reads it to you. Yes, type it into the computer while you are recording. Fortunately, we didn't raise enough funds to publish it through crowdfunding. Thank you, God. We learned a lot, in any case.

Why did we think that was a good idea? I highly recommend that you avoid that experience.

Chapter 27

We'd made plans. However, sometimes life happens, and plans undergo detours.

We'd hoped Dr. Ann could have helped us with functional medicine. She did. She helped us understand a bigger picture of what was happening within my body. Based on the lab and imaging findings, she ordered the right tests and targeted therapies that probably would have worked with ninety-five percent of the population. But, my body responded differently to the medications, particularly the hormones. That was neither her fault nor mine.

On the other hand, the failed therapies directed me to delve deeper into DreamWeaving. They also led me to meet Dr. Cua. I gained firsthand insight into the power of acupuncture and nutritional supplements formulated with whole foods. It was a therapy I didn't think could work as effectively as it did. But, after experiencing results from Dr. Cua's treatments, I know how powerful holistic therapy methods can be when applied at the right place and time.

Connections with people and animals were most therapeutic. It's within relationships that Amber and I gained support and forward movement. Our community banded together and donated hope, strength, meals, and calm when we needed it most.

Amber and I learned from each turn and challenge by facing our reality and deciding to take another route. We made many mistakes along the way. And we embraced our successes with another step forward.

DreamWeaving Notebook

Plus (+)

- We had support
- Ability to listen to instincts ⇒ serendipity
- Animals bring unconditional love, entertainment, and support
- Good verbal and non-verbal communication at work

Delta (△)

- Unknown cause(s) of symptoms
- Didn't always follow through with guidance (spiritual and otherwise)
- Lack of or inefficient use of finances

Rx

- Realize I'm worthy of love, money, and comfort
- Improve communication skills with loved ones
- Improve active listening skills
- Follow through with hard work while honoring instincts and spiritual guidance

Solution: Acknowledge current circumstances as motivation to plan and act to maintain or change them. Reciprocal support of my community.

The message of hope: Forgiveness and compassion must be present to move towards grace.

SECTION 6

GRACE

Move ~ Pray ~ Live

Chapter 28

Amber and I learned to become savvy with
our resources, leading us to grace.

My health improved while staying at my client's guest house. But Amber and Buster had lost twenty pounds during the same timeframe. All of us had gray hair and skin discolorations materializing.

Our friends were family to us. We were trying to place roots in Santa Fe. We thought we'd found our place personally and professionally. We loved our bright, comfortable home and its location. People were enthusiastic and engaged regarding DreamWeaving. My business was growing. All that hard work was paying off. However, the doors to my health and home were closing. *No Health, No Practice*, indeed. After much deliberation, we decided that our family's health was more important than taking the chance that it would decline further. We were heartbroken with the decision to uproot ourselves and move but did so, hoping we were removing the possible source of illness.

Amber and I were looking for a safe, healthy environment that was easily within our means and accepted our four pets. We looked for rentals in Santa Fe but didn't find anything within our means that suited our specific needs. After looking at several notebook pages of rental listings, Amber's finger "accidentally" opened a tab on her phone app. The rent was more than we wanted to pay, but it fit our criteria. We moved to downtown Albuquerque on December 31st, 2013.

Our moving day was wrought with challenges and blessings. Several friends had offered to bring a truck but couldn't make it. Niki showed up again. We were left with another problem to solve. How could we fit the belongings in our 1,800-square-foot house into one 2009 Subaru Outback and one 2005 Toyota Corolla?

We'd already decided only to take probably mold-spore-free things and leave the rest in our two-car garage until we could return. Amber and Niki worked inside the house while I did what I could outside.

We secured a moving truck. It was a banner of our decision that alerted those within view.

Neighbors gravitated toward us as we packed. They shared their stories when they heard we were moving due to health issues. The neighbor's father across the easement has rare spine cancer after he repaired their buckled drywall. And her sister, and roommate, experienced severe weight loss within the same timeframe. Another neighbor had unidentified and unresolved stomach pain. We heard about people who had moved because their children got sick, and doctors couldn't figure out what was wrong or how to treat them. Someone's father had passed away recently due to cancer. Another neighbor said other people in the immediate area had similar symptoms to mine. Many people in our subdivision had homes with failed roofs. Packing and moving became an enlightening glance into the lives of our neighbors and neighborhood.

We wiped off every surface before we put each representation of our hard work and nostalgia in the truck.

We started at dawn and ended well beyond dusk. Niki stuck with us from start to finish.

We were in a new place and felt hopeful for a new beginning. I'd regained strength and function during my month-long stay in the guest house and wanted to continue being proactive in my healing approach. The research I'd done showed some symptom correlation with mold exposure. But, a more substantial correlation between heavy metals, strokes, and cancer. I decided to pursue the theory that if we removed exposure to mold spores and I proactively encouraged my body to rid itself of heavy metals, I might continue to strengthen and heal. I added a minuscule amount of an herbal chelator to my supplement regime.

The next few days, I doubled over in inescapable pain. It took much effort to get up from the Thai Massage Mat that was now our bed. I felt a burning sensation inside my organs and underneath my skin. My eyes were red and burning. My hair was falling out by the handful, and I felt like I was wearing a tight shower cap. When I looked in the mirror, I noticed lumpy, hardened deposits formed underneath the skin of my face and neck. When

I looked at my abdomen, arms, and legs, I realized the deposits were global.

What started this cascade of events? More importantly, how could I change its course?

Chapter 29

Downtown Albuquerque
January 2014

There was a trail of bright red blood from the toilet to the tub. Blood was pouring out of my anus.

I don't remember transferring to the tub.

I remember using a dowel as a cane to move from the bed to the bathroom. When I sat on the toilet, blood audibly poured out of my body into the bowl. I felt extremely weak. My viscera emanated gripping pain that overcame my coping limits.

I tried everything that had previously helped me alleviate pain. I applied essential oils. I tried homeopathy. I drank California Poppy Leaf tea. I took a partial dose of Naproxen. I usually gained relief from pain by soaking in the tub, but even that wasn't working this time.

I observed the water in the tub growing deeper red as I sat there.

Amber entered the bathroom and sat next to the tub with a helpless look in her eyes. I slowly angled my head to look at her with my exhausted eyes. I thought about calling an ambulance.

I began to muffle, "I think we should call…"

"NO! Please don't die!" Amber sobbed.

I closed my eyes and said, "Will we have fun?"

She said, "Yes."

She pulled the plug on the tub and helped my limp body back to bed. As I lay there, I thought it was possible that, at this rate, I'd bleed out by morning. I felt unusual sensations, like warm liquid spilling onto my organs. I looked at my abdomen. The sensation correlated with spontaneous bruising underneath my skin. What would cause this to happen?

I couldn't get the image of sitting in bright red bathwater out of my head. Bright red blood was exiting my anus, and had been for several days when I sat down to use the restroom. Amber's plea haunted me. I couldn't get comfortable or sleep.

I turned on the tv and channel-surfed, attempting to distract my thoughts. The rabbit ears on top of our tv offered a choice of five stations. During the early morning hours, my choices were infomercials or religious programs. While Amber and our pets slept beside me, I listened to tokens of wisdom from Dr. Charles Stanley, Charles Prince, and Joyce Meyers. All three preached the same message that night. Ask for God's Grace, and it shall be granted.

I prayed from the depths of my soul, asking for God's Grace. *God, I ask for your Grace. Let me pass tonight, or show me how to heal. I promise to live my truth.*

A few moments passed. I watched a little more tv. Then, I felt a tingling sensation throughout my body. A sense of peace enveloped me and replaced the pain I'd felt. I felt a deep gratitude that I can't put words to and drifted to sleep.

The next morning, I awakened.

Chapter 30

My health allowed me to learn to live with mindfulness. I concluded there's a difference between being proactive and maintaining consistency, balance, and patience. It's the difference between healing and curing. I tried to cure my health condition by chelating heavy metals out of my tissues and into my blood so my body could eliminate those toxins. I applied a holistic modality of healing with a Western Medical mindset. It was not suitable for my body and not a sustainable way of healing for a representative of the five percent of people who heal almost exclusively using holistic means.

As long as I awakened each day, I had an opportunity to learn firsthand how the body restores homeostasis and returns to optimal function. After everything I'd experienced and read, I didn't think I could fully recover to living versus surviving. Still, I could learn more about how integrating and aligning two complementary schools of thought could promote healing.

My PCP from October 2013 referred me to an integrative medical center and a specialist, Dr. Arti Prasad. She was the Chief of Internal Medicine and

Integrative Oncology at the University of New Mexico and an Ayurvedic physician. My first appointment was on February 7, 2014, with a new PCP, a Nurse Practitioner, Cristi. I shared my health history and January tub experience with her. She had already authenticated my October 2013 test results and had someone enter the extensive list of supplements I'd been taking. Then, she ordered blood labs.

My first appointment with Dr. Prasad was on March 3, 2014. She spent more than the average nine minutes with me as her patient. (Prasad, 2012) I was in her office for over an hour while she and an Integrative Medicine intern listened to my health history. They said it was difficult to believe I could survive the events I'd described, especially without Western Medical intervention. I leaned on my cane, upgraded from the dowel I'd used, and wholeheartedly agreed. Then, released an audible sigh. When she asked me questions, I could think of what I wanted to say but couldn't physically form and speak the words. That symptom and word find got progressively worse after each transient ischemic event.

She wanted to order tests and therapies that would require pharmaceuticals. I declined the colonoscopy due to the drugs but agreed to a stool test. The February 7th tests showed that I no longer had occult blood in my stool. I shared that I'd added one of Dr. Cua's formulations to fortify my bones, skin, and hair. That, combined with drinking chocolate milk, helped decrease bruising, pain, and subcutaneous burning sensations. I wanted to refrain from taking pharmaceuticals if possible, and I had to respect what my body could and couldn't tolerate.

She released an audible sigh. I told her I wasn't trying to be difficult. She thanked me for acknowledging the challenge my case presented. I greatly appreciated her flexibility and ingenuity in navigating a complex health condition within my body's parameters and tolerance.

There were, however, a few issues that required immediate attention. The most urgent were breast masses, hypothyroidism, and pain and energy management. I opted out of biopsies and agreed to monitor the masses with mammograms and diagnostic ultrasounds every six months. I wanted to attempt to remedy my hypothyroidism with Dr. Cua's herbal supplements. She said it couldn't be done, but I wasn't drastically out of normal range. She agreed to see what the next blood tests revealed. She also recommended that I take vitamin D3. I agreed. Then, I told her that if my next tests showed that I worsened, I would take her recommended pharmaceuticals.

Dr. Prasad referred me to an acupuncturist, Dr. Smith. She was a nurse who studied acupuncture in China and specialized in chronic pain. I agreed to see Dr. Smith.

I felt hopeful again. Intuitively, I knew I was in the right place at the right time.

I'd promised God and myself that I'd live my truth. I didn't know how that would play out. My team of providers monitored my health. I took responsibility for my health by making it a point to be my best advocate while my doctors tried to pinpoint diagnoses and figure out how to help me without using drugs. I had a mammogram, diagnostic ultrasound every six months, and follow-up blood tests. In June 2014, my thyroid levels were within normal limits by adding Dr. Cua's supplements and consistent DreamWeaving Aromatherapy Applications. Dr. Prasad tested me for everything she could think of; Hashimoto's disease, HIV, Hepatitis, and rheumatoid, etc. I had more tests in December 2014 and May 2015. We all worked together on the diagnostic process while avoiding all pharmaceuticals and tried to learn from my healing process.

Finally, my team of providers said that whatever was going on with my health wasn't in any book. None of my symptoms perfectly aligned with anything we had read about. We were all perplexed. They'd witnessed a transient ischemic attack in their office on June 3, 2014, when they called emergency personnel. We kept trying.

I had been doing everything by the book while Amber did what she felt. Aside from losing twenty pounds during December, she seemed to be faring better. Why? She ate what she craved when she craved it and rested when she felt tired. She was following her body's cues while I was leaning more heavily on the current norms of health. Perhaps those norms applied to a healthy body, but a health challenge might require individualized and specific changes in diet and lifestyle.

New information continues to surface as technology advances, but we still need to understand many things.

Maybe my best bets and bites were following my intuition and eating what I craved.

I took inventory of patterns that exacerbated and relieved the symptoms. Stress and anger always correlated with the heightening of my symptoms. Having fun and feeling at ease always helped decrease stress. I needed to heal some festering emotional wounds from the past to regain strength and health. Every cell of my body craved homeostasis.

Since nobody could figure out the cause of my symptoms and inability to metabolize drugs, I changed my perspective from curing unknown diagnoses and focused on finding a healing solution. Authentic interests led me to more helpful information as long as I could discern what was applicable and what wasn't. If I didn't heal, my doctors might better understand natural disease progression without the interference of drugs. As a physician, it would be a way for me to fulfill my purpose of promoting the understanding of holistic healing. I had to keep trying. If and when something I did had a positive effect, I'd attempt to figure out why it worked. I called it reverse research. If I understood the mechanism of action better, I could postulate my next hypothesis and choices more accurately. I combined subjective and objective information and aligned my choices with science and time-honored wisdom.

It was all speculation until there was empirical data. I was glad I'd requested to be tested for heavy metals the previous October. Sharing the information from those tests after a DreamWeaving Certification Course class prompted my friend, Isabella, to give me articles to read that stated heavy metals tended to mimic calcium. During the American Veterinary Chiropractic Association convention, a veterinarian friend told me that heavy metals had an affinity for protein and fat. They tend to get deposited directly into the skin, hair, organs, and tissues. (Gupta, 2012) According to the CDC, chelating one heavy metal is dangerous and could cause kidney failure. That was the rule rather than the exception. Was it possible to chelate gently? Was it possible that the normal limits of metals within the blood were the body's way of discerning what was safe to eliminate with a global check and balance using the built-in negative feedback system?

There was much information, yet there were still no answers. Where did the heavy metals in my blood come from? They were within the normal limit range. However, that accepted value had changed over the years. Was there one source or many sources? Was there an unidentified diagnosis? Was I exposed to environmental toxins? I didn't know. I continued to look for patterns.

I still wondered if building materials had anything to do with my condition. While having dinner with family members in Albuquerque and sharing my symptom picture with them, the Florida contractor asked if I had been exposed to faulty drywall. He said my symptoms were consistent with what he saw in Florida when it was widely used. I told him I didn't know.

I discovered the Material Safety Data Sheet (MSDS) for drywall. I read that exposure to water could change its safety due to chemical release. I looked a little deeper as to why. When water was added to sulfur dioxide, it yielded sulfuric acid. Drywall contains sulfur dioxide. And sulfur has a yellow hue. We had yellow dust in our home after the drywall buckled in our garage. I read that water added to sulfur dioxide could cause a severe burning sensation. As I read on, I wondered why there were known carcinogens in drywall.

I researched more and tried to get the big picture of my symptoms and possible causes.

I'd salivated profusely when I was south of Siler Road in Santa Fe but not north of that location. I'd witnessed a few dogs salivate due to toxicity while I did DreamWeaving sessions. Was that a natural response to a toxin for all species? If so, which one, or ones? Gypsum? Something else?

There were so many moving pieces.

Then, one day, I listened to a TV show in the background while steaming vegetables for the dogs. I heard the narrator mention similar symptoms to mine. Someone was poisoned with arsenic. They felt fatigued and had digestive disorders, skin changes, and bleeding. Plus, they were completely aware while all of that was happening. The picture of symptoms was so similar to mine that I stopped what I was doing and walked into the other room to listen more closely.

Synchronicity makes life interesting.

DreamWeaving Notebook

Plus (+)

- Awareness of a higher power/God and spirit guides
- Dedication to education and knowledge
- A natural inclination to investigate further

Delta (△)

- Self-doubt
- Needed better empirical data
- Loss of integrity of my endothelium and epithelium, i.e., skin
- We needed better communication skills at home and with our neighbors

Rx

- Remain loyal to my truth and purpose
- Believe in infinite possibilities
- Be confident with my actions

Solution: Have faith!

The message of hope: God's guidance and grace are omnipresent.

References

178natfue. (2012, November 2). *The Soul's Whip* [Video file]. Retrieved from https://www.youtube.com/watch?v=z4-jwMev0.

Breslau, Naomi, Kessler, R.C. (2001). The stressor criterion in DSM-IV Post traumatic stress disorder: An empirical investigation. *Biological Psychiatry, 50(9), 699-709.* http://dx.doi.org/10.1016/S0006-3223(01)01167-2.

Christensen, Jen. (2015, Feb 11). A third of Americans use alternative medicine. *CNN.* Retrieved from http://www.cnn.com/2015/02/11/health/feat-alternative-medicine-study/.

Cuddy, Amy J.C.; Wilmuth, Caroline A.; Carney, Dana R. "The Benefit of Power Posing Before High-Stakes Social Evaluation." Harvard Business School Working Paper, No. 13-027, September 2012. Accessed February 11, 2018 11:32:54am EST http://nrs.harvard.edu/urn-3:HUL.InstRepos:9547823.

Dunn, Adam (2000, Dec 21). 'Kokology' plays self-discovery games with your brain. *CNN*. Retrieved from www.cnn.com/2000/books/news/12/21/kokology.book/.

Higley, Connie and Alan (2010). Reference Guide for Essential Oils, Twelfth Edition. Spanish Fork, Utah: Abundant Health.

Gupta, Ramesh C. (2012). Veterinary Toxicology: Basic and Clinical Principles, second edition. 346-348. San Diego, CA: Elsevier. Retrieved from https://books.google.com/books?isbn=0123859271.

Memme, J.M., Erlich, A.T., Phukan, G. and Hood, D. A. (2021). Exercise and Mitochondrial health. *Journal of Physiology*. 599:803-817. https://doi.org/10.1113/JP278853.

Mojay, Gabriel (1997). Aromatherapy for Healing the Spirit. Rochester, Vermont: Healing Arts Press.

Patwardhan, Shashikant, Patwardhan, Sushama. (2002). Ayurvedic Technique of Pulse Diagnosis. Retrieved from https://ayurveda-foryou.com/clinical_ayurveda/pulse_diagnosis.html.

Prasad, Dr. Arti; Walhof, Dr. Debbie; Burke, Dr. Kathi. (2012, October 28). 9 minutes. *TEDx Talks*. Retrieved from https://youtube.com/watch?v=JFaelEULTc.

Pugachevsky, Julia. (2014, April 22). This "Cube" personality test will absolutely blow your mind: Can you handle the truth? *Buzz Feed*. Retrieved from https://www.buzzfeed.com/juliapugachevsky/these-questions-will-tell-you-everything-you-need-to-know?utm_term=.muQ0D7aLM#.fxNJr7aG0Q.

Rendon, Jim. (2015, Jul 22). How trauma can change you - for the better. *Time*. Retrieved from time.com/3967885/how-truama-can-change-you-for-the-better/.

Stussman, Barbara J., Black, Lindsey I., Clark, Tainya C., Nahin, Richard L. (2015, Nov 4). Wellness-related use of common complementary health approaches among adults: United States, 2012. *National Health Statistics Report*. 85. Retrieved from https://www.cdc.gov/nchs/data/nhsr/nhsr085.pdf.

Tadeschi, R.G., Calhoun, L.G. (1996). The Posttraumatic Growth Inventory: Measuring the positive legacy of trauma. *Journal of Traumatic Stress*. Jul: 9(3), 455-471.

Worwood, Valerie Ann (1999). Aromatherapy for the Soul. Novato, California: New World Library.

Appendix 1

DreamWeaving Holographic Health Curriculum Overview

Touch the soul

Guide the mind
Comfort the body
Elevate your senses
Live your truth

DreamWeaving Holographic Health is an innovative aromatherapy application to lifestyle choices and practices. Allopathic wellness concepts align with traditional holistic systems of harmonious living to offer an insightful and dynamic wellness experience.

Certified DreamWeaving practitioners undergo rigorous training to ensure they embody wellness so they may apply holographic healing principles through a clear body and mind.

All levels are welcome. There is no pre-requisite for the Level 1 course. Attendees must pass self-care, written, practical, and bridge exams for Level 1 and each subsequent level to progress to the next course of study.

LEVEL 1 - LEVITY - *Lighthearted awareness lifts consciousness*
This is a general introduction to DreamWeaving philosophy. A perspective of unity of the body/mind and inclusion is embodied in a light-hearted atmosphere.

LEVEL 2 - AND - *Connectivity allows synergistic flow*
Verbal and non-verbal communication is the key to understanding internal and external interactions. Exponential benefits of the two(2)-person and 2-system aligned approach are explored.

LEVEL 3 - DreamWeaving Fitness (DWF) - *Dynamic balance*
Experience the importance of remaining grounded while developing, recognizing, and utilizing instincts. We'll employ the poetry of motion.

LEVEL 4 - POWER - *Authentic presence fuels exponential influence*
This course provides the framework to open your heart and mind to your truth. Forward movement towards living your most authentic life is encouraged.

LEVEL 5 - THROUGH - *Trust the process*
This course has themes of honesty, mindfulness, focus, goals, and resilience.

LEVEL 6 - GRACE - *Move ~ Pray ~ Live*

Making choices based on observation of natural laws and giving science equal weight as instinct allow us to hone our skills into a complete package. We put in the last piece of the puzzle.

LEVEL 7 - CAPSTONE CLASS/INDIVIDUALIZED INTERNSHIP - *Bloom and Grow*

We meet as a class to refine our skills and share experiences of the internship. Each individual develops specific skills to apply DreamWeaving Holographic Health to their truth.

Topics vary. All skills learned up to this point are applied to real-life situations.

Each exam consists of a four-part process: Self-Care, written, practical, and bridge exams. Practitioners must pass an exit exam following the internship to become a Certified DreamWeaving Holographic Health Certified practitioner.

Appendix 2

Table 1 - Chemistry of Essential Oils

Chemical Groups	Name of Compound	General Effect	Oil Example
Hydrocarbons	Monoterpenes (-ene)	Help discharge existing toxins from the liver and kidneys	Most citrus oils
	Sesquiterpenes (-ene)	Liver and gland stimulants; crosses blood-brain barrier	Cedarwood, Copaiba, Palo Santo
Oxygenated Compounds	Alcohols (-ol)	Revert cells to normal function and activity; uplifting, generally safe	Geranium, Lemon
	Esters (-yl -ate)	Most calming, balancing, and relaxing, especially on the nervous system	Roman Chamomile, Helichrysum, Jasmine
	Aldehydes (-al, -aldehyde)	Calming to emotions and CNS; can be irritating to skin	Cinnamon Bark, Lemongrass
	Ketones (-one)	Stimulate cell regeneration; liquefy mucous	Hyssop, Sage, Spearmint
	Phenols (-ol)	Most powerful anti-bacterial; immune and NS stimulating; can be caustic to skin or hepatotoxic in large doses	Clove, Oregano, Peppermint
	Oxides (-ol, -oxide)	Expectorants; mildly stimulating	Myrtle, Dorado Azul, Rosemary (CT cineol)

Appendix 3

Table 2 - Jackie's DreamWeaving Technique Chart

Dates	Essential Oil Application (Number of drops, oil)	Reason(s) For Essential Oil Use	Disbanding (Area/Region)
9/08/2011	3, *Foeniculum vulgare (Fennel)* diluted with 1t. fractionated coconut oil	(Monoterpenes) may help break up fluids & toxins & cleanse tissues.[1] Bring hidden issues to light, provide protection from outside influences, perseverance.[3]	Occiput Cervical Thoracic Lumbar Sacral
9/13/2011	5, *Origanum majorana (Marjoram)* neat	Support for spleen, "digestion", and muscles.[1] Ease anxiety, restore *qi* of spleen-pancreas, regulating effect on the *Yi*.[2]	Parietal Cervical Thoracic Sacral
9/22/2011	3, EndoFlex™ blend 6, Marjoram neat	EndoFlex™-Endocrine support, thyroid regulation, discharge of toxins, helps to burn up fats and toxins.[1] Marjoram-Help release idea that "no one cares".[2]	Cervical Thoracic Lumbar Sacral Coccyx

Table 2 - Jackie's DreamWeaving Technique Chart

Dates	Essential Oil Application (Number of drops, oil)	Reason(s) For Essential Oil Use	Disbanding (Area/Region)
9/28/2011	5, Valor™ blend 3, Marjoram "petted" neat along spine	Valor-Assist in aligning and balancing physical structure, build courage, confidence, & help revert anaerobic cells back to aerobic natural state.[1] (Marjoram-see above)	Cervical Thoracic Lumbar Sacral Left Scapula
10/05/2011	5, Valor™ blend 3, *Citrus x paradisi* (Grapefruit) 1, *Citrus sinensis* (Orange) "rubbed in" neat over spleen region 3, Di-Gize™ blend neat thoracic and lumbar regions	(Valor-See above) Grapefruit-d-limonene's anti-tumoral effects, support for the lymphatic system.[1] Orange-"brings happiness to the heavyhearted and those who seem lost".[3] Di-Gize™ to help him "digest" toxins & emotions that may emerge.	Cervical Thoracic Lumbar Sacral
10/12/2011	2, *Syzygium aromaticum* (Clove) 3, *Cymbopogon flexuosus* (Lemongrass) 2, Valor™ 2, Di-Gize™ all applied neat over spleen region	Clove-anti-tumoral, anti-inflammatory effects, & immune stimulant.[1] Lemongrass-to help him "forgive then forget".[3] Valor™ & Di-Gize™-(See above).	N/A

Table 2 - Jackie's DreamWeaving Technique Chart

Dates	Essential Oil Application (Number of drops, oil)	Reason(s) For Essential Oil Use	Disbanding (Area/Region)
10/18/2011	5, 3 Wise Men™ blend "petted" neat over area of spleen	3 Wise Men™- facilitate the release of negative emotions & keep them from reattaching to the body.[1]	Cervical Thoracic Lumbar Sacral Left Ilium
10/26/2011	6 passes, Past Tense™ roll-on 2, *Coriandrum sativum* (Coriander) "petted" neat on thoracolumbar region	Past Tense™ blend- endocrine support. Coriander-centering- pancreatic support and therefore, support for all Earth Element organs, including the spleen.	Cervical Thoracic Sacral
11/02/2011	1, Brain Power™ blend neat on lesion on Right temporal region 5 passes, Past Tense™ blend 3, Coriander "petted" neat on spine	Brain Power™-for it's powerfully uplifting and energizing aroma.[1] Past Tense™ blend and Coriander (See above).	Cervical Thoracic Sacral
11/23/2011	2 passes, Past Tense™ blend 2, EndoFlex™ blend "petted" neat on spine	Past Tense™ blend & EndoFlex™ blend- endocrine support.	Cervical Thoracic Lumbar Sacral Left Posterior ribs (2-4) Left Ilium

Table References: 1 - Higley 2010, 2 - Mojay 1997, 3 - Worwood 1999

Printed in the United States
by Baker & Taylor Publisher Services